JUN   2014

DISCARDED

The Happy Life Checklist

THOUSAND OAKS LIBRARY
1401 E. Janss Road
Thousand Oaks, California

DISCARDED

The Happy Life
Checklist

654 Little Things
That Will Bring You Bliss

Amy Spencer

A PERIGEE BOOK

A PERIGEE BOOK
Published by the Penguin Group
Penguin Group LLC
375 Hudson Street, New York, New York 10014

USA • Canada • UK • Ireland • Australia • New Zealand • India • South Africa • China

penguin.com

A Penguin Random House Company

Copyright © 2014 by Amy Spencer
Penguin supports copyright. Copyright fuels creativity, encourages diverse voices,
promotes free speech, and creates a vibrant culture. Thank you for buying an authorized
edition of this book and for complying with copyright laws by not reproducing, scanning,
or distributing any part of it in any form without permission. You are supporting writers
and allowing Penguin to continue to publish books for every reader.
PERIGEE is a registered trademark of Penguin Group LLC.
The "P" design is a trademark belonging to Penguin Group LLC.

Library of Congress Cataloging-in-Publication Data

Spencer, Amy, 1971–
The happy life checklist : 654 simple ways to find your bliss / Amy Spencer.— First edition.
p.   cm.
ISBN 978-0-399-16556-6 (pbk.)
1. Happiness.   2. Positive psychology.   3. Optimism.   I. Title.
BF575.H27.S74   2014
158.1—dc23   2013033107

First edition: February 2014

PRINTED IN THE UNITED STATES OF AMERICA

10 9 8 7 6 5 4 3 2 1

Text design by Kristin del Rosario

While the author has made every effort to provide accurate telephone numbers,
Internet addresses, and other contact information at the time of publication, neither the
publisher nor the author assumes any responsibility for errors, or for changes that occur
after publication. Further, the publisher does not have any control over and does not
assume any responsibility for author or third-party websites or their content.

Most Perigee books are available at special quantity discounts for bulk purchases for sales
promotions, premiums, fund-raising, or educational use. Special books, or book excerpts, can also
be created to fit specific needs. For details, write: Special.Markets@us.penguingroup.com.

For my friends,

the wildflowers of my life.

CONTENTS

1. ## VITALITY   1

Bringing out your healthiest self in the big,
bright world

2. ## WONDER   23

Savoring the present moment, mindful of the
beautiful now

3. ## COMFORT   41

Creating a cozy, beautiful life; at home,
wherever you are

CONTENTS

I was sitting in an Adirondack chair in my backyard on a Saturday afternoon, wearing my Panama hat and reading a good book in the sunshine. My husband walked up behind me and started rubbing my shoulders. It was just a few nice little squeezes, so I closed my eyes and breathed in the moment. I wanted to inhale those bright seconds of bliss, to take a mental snapshot in time, with a caption that would have read: *This is happiness.*

"Mmmm," I said. "Happy capture."

"Happy what?" he asked.

"I don't know," I said. "This is a perfect little burst of happiness. I want to capture and remember it." Life was giving me a little squeeze, and my heart was hugging it back.

And we all have opportunities to take in the small things like this every day; in fact, life is teeming with them: curtains

billowing in the **breeze** through city windows, a **sunlit surfboard** on the sand, friends **laughing**, a **fresh** plate of **handmade** pasta, an architectural **marvel**, a **puppy** playing in the **grass**, a steaming **cappuccino**, a **tangerine**-colored **taxi**, cute **kids** leaping on a **fluffy** white **bed**, an **antique** book, a **snowcapped** mountain, a **tropical** island. Life provides us with instant snapshots of what happiness is every day. The only problem? We don't always see it.

It reminds me of the *Washington Post* experiment, about how much of life's beauty we take in. On an early January morning in 2007, concert violinist Joshua Bell planted himself inside a set of doors at the Metro station in Washington, DC. He took out his violin, placed the open case in front of him for tips, and began to play "Chaconne," from Bach's Partita No. 2 in D Minor, which Bell called, "Not just one of the greatest pieces of music ever written, but one of the greatest achievements of any man in history." Bell was recorded by a hidden camera, so the newspaper could see how many people would stop to listen to this Grammy Award–winning musician performing incognito.

It turned out, as writer Gene Weingarten discovered, of the more than one thousand people who passed by Bell in those forty-five minutes, only *seven* stopped to listen—and one because she recognized him. If you watch the video posted online, you'll see what so many of us do every day: people rushing past because they have a meeting to keep, a train to make, groceries to buy, people to see. Either they don't feel they have time to listen to a masterfully elegant violin performance, or they're so focused on their destination, they don't even hear it.

So just like we might ask, "If a tree falls in a forest but no one hears it, does it really make a sound?" I'll throw out this one: If a day bursts full of potentially bright moments but you don't notice a single one of them, do they really count?

What Is a Happy Life?

If you could pick one big thing that you think would make you happier, what might it be? I've been asking people that "big" question for eight months now and taking notes. Some things I've heard:

"A big kitchen with a huge island in the center."

"A silver Porsche Boxster."

"Ugh, losing all the weight I gained when I turned forty."

"A vacation in one of those huts on the water in Fiji."

"A partner in love. Someone in my life so I don't feel like a complete reject. Anyone? Anyone?"

"One hundred million dollars. Wrapped around a kitten."

We all have our own vision of how to reach that crest of happiness, where we can look out over the vista of our life and say, finally, *This is it. I'm happy.* And it often includes the types of things mentioned above—big milestones we dream of achieving. And those things *will* make us happy for a while. But as research in positive psychology has shown, they actually won't keep us happy for very long.

We can thank our tendency toward "habituation" or "hedonic adaptation" for that. The problem is, as soon as we get that one big thing, we start to get used to it. We appreciate our new car for as long as it retains that "new car smell," but climbing into the front seat eventually becomes such a regular habit, it no longer impresses us. We human beings are simply very good at adjusting to our circumstances. That's beneficial when we're adapting back to life's set point after a breakup, an illness, or a job loss—when something bad has happened to us. But we also get used to the *good* things, too. It doesn't matter how stunning something is the first time we see it; once it becomes a habit, we simply start tuning it out. So if we spend our lives only reaching for the next "big" thing ahead of us, we will never feel truly happy.

In fact, as research by positive psychologists has found, *only about 10 percent* of our happiness is based on those "big" things anyway: our money, our home, or the town where we live. If you were to trade your life for someone else's today—someone with a "better" mate, a "better" job, and a "better" house in a "better" place—you'd only be a *smidge* happier. It seems nuts, but it's true. Those billionaires? They're simply not all that much happier than we are.

One famous study led by Ed Diener, PhD, showed that Americans earning more than $10 million a year reported being only moderately happier than those whose mean family income was $36,000. Numerous studies on lottery winners have found that having more money sometimes made them *less* happy. And another study found that material purchases just don't make us as happy as enduring life experiences do. Also surprising: When Diener and his researchers asked the wealthy people what it was that made them happy, they didn't mention their swimming pools and yachts. They mentioned happy family relationships, good health, and feeling fulfilled by helping others.

We don't get happy by reaching for extrinsic goals *outside* of ourselves; happiness comes intrinsically, from *within* us. It isn't what we have that matters, it's how we *feel* about what we have. It isn't what happens to us that matters, it's how we *experience* what happens to us. It isn't what's in front of us that matters, it's how we *see* what's in front of us. We don't have to win the lottery to be rich; the riches of life are at our fingertips every single day. We just have to train ourselves to tune in to them.

Seeing Life Through Kid-Colored Lenses

Remember how summer seemed to go on forever when you were young? It felt like six months of playing outdoors, going to camp, swimming, bike riding, hitting the beach, or playing stickball in the street. And now? Sheesh, Labor Day has come and gone before we know it.

That's because the way our brains work, the more emotionally charged a situation is, the more it's stamped deep into our emotional brains. This is why you don't forget your most gushing first love, your most embarrassing moment, your most heartwrenching breakup, or your scariest accident. The bigger the emotion—be it happiness, guilt, fear, love, excitement—the bigger the effect.

Because kids are new to life, they're getting a lot of emotionally charged input every day, so their days seem bigger and fuller than ours. It's as if kids are watching their life movie in slow motion, taking in every frame, while we, on the other hand, are watching ours on fast-forward with the volume muted. We've already seen it all before, so thanks to habituation, we don't even notice the good stuff anymore.

Which means if we want to appreciate those things again, we have to consciously tune back in and see life through a child's eyes again. If we can appreciate the fun we're having each day, our whole year can feel like a big, long summer. Fitness trainer Jillian Michaels once said, "Transformation is not a future event. It is a present activity." I love that idea because it also applies to transforming your feelings about your life. Happiness isn't a future event; it's a present activity. It isn't about crossing the finish line of that one big goal ahead; it's about feeling your feet on the pavement as you take each step. If you show up for your life in small ways every day, you will get closer to bliss.

Singer/songwriter Christine Lavin wrote a song about babysitting a three-year-old named Katy. After dancing in the living room together, the little girl beamed, "Today is the best day of my whole entire life." Christine was so pleased with herself, she told Katy's parents, thinking they'd be as impressed with her babysitting skills as she was. Instead, they smiled. Katy, they told her, had said the same thing yesterday; in fact, they added, "Lately, she's been saying that every day." I love that story, because, my gosh, shouldn't *we* be saying that every day? Today can be the best day of *your* whole entire life, as long as you build your day around the right things. And the funny thing for me is that it took a day of doing it all *wrong* to figure out how we can fix it.

How to Build a Happy Life Checklist

One day last fall, I got through nearly everything on my to-do list for the third or fourth day in a row. I'd handed in all of my assignments, sent all my emails, paid all my bills, and then I set out a new plan to do it again the next day. I felt very accomplished, sure, but I didn't necessarily feel *happy*. Because in order to get everything done, I had holed myself up in my office, had barely seen my husband, didn't speak with my friends, ate poorly, and the only exercise I got was through my fingertips typing at the computer. And when I started making my list for the next day, I just saw more of the same: calls to make, research to do, appointments to book. Where was all the fun stuff? And then it hit me: The fun stuff wasn't getting done *because it wasn't on the list*. I had prioritized my day through little check boxes on paper. But in doing so, I had put my relationships, my health, and my rest at the bottom of it! Essentially, I was living a happy life upside down.

That's what got me thinking about how unbalanced most of our to-do lists really are, how we weigh down our days with things we dread before we've even had our morning coffee. We needed, I decided, a new kind of list. And I knew just where to turn for inspiration: the small Himalayan kingdom of Bhutan.

Bhutan, nestled between China and India, has become known for being the first country in the world to measure their Gross National Happiness (GNH). Over the past few decades, country leaders, overseen by the Centre for Bhutan Studies, have developed a measure of happiness based on elements like living standards, psychological well-being, good governance, education, health, and ecology. To increase their GNH, they work on small changes within each of those domains. For instance, in the area of ecology, Bhutan banned plastic bags; and to impact education and psychological well-being, they conduct a morning meditation in their schools. By making a conscious effort to improve each individual area of importance, they rounded out their lives in a more perfect balance.

And that's how I've learned about one of the biggest keys to happiness: *balance*. You know why a piano chord sounds so beautiful? Because it's not just one beautiful note, it's three or five all played at the same time in harmony; it's some high notes mixed with some low. Why do we call a person "one note"? Because while they may have nailed one area of expertise, they seem to be missing all the rest. Balance in life comes through the full orchestra: It's the high flute playing with the low bass drum. It's the quick tempo paired with the slow. And it's a day full of things that you *have* to get done, paired with delicious items you simply *want* to.

So that fall day, when I made my new to-do list, I planned it like a gymnastics all-around. In addition to the must-dos, I added my *choose*-to-dos. I was going to round out my day in true, beautiful balance.

First, I came up with those necessary things that would feed me—literally, by working so I could bring home the bacon. It included stuff like:

☐ Email editor
☐ Buy printer ink
☐ Hand in work assignment
☐ Pay cell phone bill

Then I thought bigger, about what would feed my mind, feed my heart, feed my health, and feed my dreams. That included things like:

- [ ] Take a brisk walk to the beach and back
- [ ] Hug my husband
- [ ] Read a novel on front porch for fifteen minutes
- [ ] Tell my mom I love her

And that first day after I accomplished the items on my *new* to-do list, I felt all-around happier than I had in months. I had not only completed the necessary stuff but I had also fed my dreams, nurtured my relationships, and nourished my body.

Our lives don't have to be hamster wheels of one thing; they can be open roads full of everything. If happiness is something you want, you must make it something you actually *do*. Decide with conviction that each day *will* contain joy, that your love life *will* have a happy ending, and that you *will* thrive— and then put it on the list! Your regular to-do list covers the grind of everything you must get done. Your Happy Life Checklist covers the things you *want* to do. Rather than sit back and let life happen to you, choose to actively add elements of happiness from the book to your life. And here's the fun part: What those elements are is all up to *you*.

The Elements of Bliss

If you like the idea of building happy items into your daily to-do list, like I did, here's one way to approach it: Give yourself fifteen minutes of silence with yourself—in a park, in your bedroom, on a walk—and really think about the areas of your life you want to nourish. Ask yourself: "Which area am I missing the most right now?" and "Which category of bliss could I add more of to my life?"

If you want to be open to healthy adventures that get your blood pumping, pluck a few fresh ideas for living with **vitality**. If you want to open your eyes in awe of nature around you, seek more **wonder**. If you miss the feeling of nestling into a comfortable couch in self-care, seek **comfort**. If life is too serious and you could use some silly downtime, dip into the fun of life's **delight**. If you want to reach for your dreams, try **thriving**. If you want more love in your life, *be* more **love**. If you could use some reminders of how remarkably amazing you are, give yourself a few kicks in the butt of **confidence**. If you're always on the go, drop your head onto the pillow of **tranquility**. If you want to engage more in the cornerstone of the community around you, seek ideas of **effervescence**. And if you want to give back and gain meaning, to offer the world even more than you take in return, try **grace**.

Within each category of bliss in the book are small items, each one with its own check box. So, just as you'd complete a to-do list item of making a phone call or mopping a floor, you can also look someone directly in the eyes for three seconds when you say thank you. Throughout each section, you'll also find larger check boxes with ideas for happy life *practices* you can try to work into your life on a more regular basis; the better you get at them, the happier you'll feel more often.

Some of the ideas in this book are reminders of things you might already appreciate, like a friend's chuckle that is so funny, it makes *you* laugh every time. Other items are things happening around you that you might not be tuned in to, but which are worth paying attention to, like the satisfied feeling of pouring that first cup of coffee from a full, fresh pot. Still others are suggestions for new things to try—surprising twists to make routine life more interesting and fun.

Once you start adding these items to your own Happy Life Checklist, you'll start to experience what I call the clean-a-car-before-you-sell-it syndrome. That's what happens when you decide it's time to sell your car (or your couch or your lamp or your computer). Picture it: You've had that baby for years, and it's been good to you, but you're ready for something new. So you spend hours cleaning that vehicle inside and out: You vacuum the seats, hose down the mats, clear out the trunk, give it a wax, and replace the missing radio button on the dash. Then you stand back to see how shiny it will look to potential buyers. And that's about when you ask yourself this question: *Wait . . . why have I been driving it the other way all this time when I could have been driving this? Why,* you think, *didn't I do all this before?*

That's what this book is for. To get you spiffing up the life you have in front of you so you can see it in all its glory. As you'll come to see, you don't need big new things in your life; you just need to wash the mats, fix a few knobs, and shine it up so you can see what a gem it already is. And you know what's even cooler about your life than a car? That just *thinking* about some of these happy-spiffing ideas can create the same positive effects as actually *doing* them.

There was, for instance, a 2004 study out of the Cleveland Clinic that found weight lifters who visualized mental contractions of some small muscles for twelve weeks still increased their muscle strength by almost *half* as much as the participants who actually lifted weights. That's because visualizing an activity can engage the same cognitive functions as the times when you're actually *experiencing* them. Which means that even if you don't have access to some things on this list, it may still make you just as happy to *imagine* that you do. If you can picture yourself standing on a rock jetty looking out to boats on the horizon, the wind on your cheeks, you can still get a sense of peace from your imaginary perch. If you just think about jumping on a trampoline or drinking a cold, fizzy soda, or watching a bird soar quietly overhead, it will almost feel as if you'd been there. Hey, would ya look at that: happiness before you've really "done" a thing.

Which is why I want to say this: Don't think of this book as a required to-do list you have to slog through. Because if you're anything like me, even if the list is super-fun—like movies I've lined up on my Netflix list, or a craft project I want to dive into—it can still feel overwhelming! So rest assured: *The Happy Life Checklist* isn't about giving you more work; it's about helping you tap into more joy. *So read and use this book however you'd like*: You can read it cover to cover, checking off things you've done, and marking the ideas you want to try first. You can leave it on your bedside and flip through it at random when you want a small burst of happy inspiration. Or you can skim through the book for a little zing, because sometimes just reading positive words can make you feel brighter. Trust me: Any ideas that seem most right for you will bubble up to the surface like fat in a soup. So the next time you find yourself in a coffee shop on your way to see a friend, maybe you'll grab an extra cup to surprise them, or if someone offers you a Hula-Hoop, you'll actually step into it and give it a whirl. Have faith that however you approach this book, the little things that are right for you will soak in.

You can't change other people and you can't always change your circumstances, but you *do* have the power to change how you think, what you see, and how you feel. The choice is always up to you. You can be happy if you choose to be.

Be Happy, Now

I want you to know that as I wrote this book, I also did my best to *live* it. I didn't want to write about ideas I wasn't making an effort to experience for myself. So I ate rainbows of food, I put my feet in the water, I hugged people for two seconds longer, and I played "closet roulette" to wear things I'd forgotten I owned and loved. And the people close to me, it turns out, got in the habit of thinking that very same way. I noticed that one night, when I climbed into bed and told my husband he'd stolen my good pillow for his side of the bed.

"This one is too hard," I said. "I like the other one."

"Shouldn't you like *all* the pillows on the bed?" he asked. "That should be in the book."

He was right, we *should* like all the pillows on our bed, and it *should* have been in the book! Which is why you'll find that reminder for bliss in the **comfort** section. The point is, I intentionally did my best to live the happy life I write about here. In fact, many of these words were typed on my iPhone as I sat on the swinging bench in my backyard by the lemon tree, or as I petted my cat or took a long walk or after I'd caught up with my friends over a good meal. I wanted to make sure these words came from a truly warm and happy place, and that you feel this for yourself each time you pick up the book, and—I hope—as you start to work some of them into your life. I hope the "happy captures" I came up with will inspire you to come up with and treasure your own.

Slow down like a kid in the summer and see each small frame of your day for what it can be. *Do not underestimate the value of small things.* Small is amazing. Small is what gets us step by step along the Great Wall of China. Small is how much an oak tree grows every day from a sapling to a towering majesty. And small, in a way, is better than big. Because we're more likely to help a friend carry a small chair into their new home than agree to help move three packed stories' worth of stuff; and we're more likely to make a small change overnight than a big one. You may not get a big week's vacation napping your days away on tropical sand, but you may have the small comfort of a soft couch, moonlight on the rooftops, and fresh fruit for breakfast. *Small is the seconds and the minutes of life instead of the years.*

The Happy Life Checklist is all about those small moments—because happiness isn't up ahead of you. It's right here, in the now. It's in the hundreds of small good things you have at your fingertips every day, like yummy little gumballs from the candy machine of life. So see which sweet experiences you can start checking off on your bright new life list today.

The Happy Life Checklist

ONE

Vitality

Life is so **full** of joy, if your eyes and arms are **open** to the **adventure**. **Nourish** yourself with these **healthy** ideas. Each of them is meant to inspire you to get your **body** moving, your muscles **awake**, your spirit **refreshed**, and feel **vibrant** and at your best.

☐ **Juice it.** The orange. The apple. The grapefruit. If you don't have your own juicer, have a local market make one for you. Drink the sweet sap of fresh flavor—from the fruit, to the glass, to you.

☐ **Work up a sweat.** The kind that trickles from your forehead and wets your belly. It feels good to work hard enough—in the gym, the garden, on the dance floor—that your body is dripping with proof.

☐ **Brush your teeth with your other hand.** Outsmart your "novelty detector neurons" that tune out the routine things in your life by mixing up the most routine thing you do every day.

☐ **Blindfold yourself while you eat.** Some restaurants offer the chance to dine in complete darkness so you can experience what it's like to eat without your sense of sight. Try it at home: Wrap a scarf over your eyes and see how it enhances the flavors and textures dancing on your palate when you're not distracted by anything else. With one of your major senses blocked, you will tune in more with the rest.

☐ **Sit by a fire.** Gather around a fire pit in the backyard. Grill food over a camping flame. Or sit beside an indoor fireplace or a heater that feels like one. Let the warmth or glow envelop you.

☐ **Amp up your shower.** Spring for the shampoo that smells so good you get happy. Choose a bright new body puff. A colorful bath mat. Or a tiny plant that lives for the light and steam.

☐ **Plant an herb in view of where you spend the most time.** Instead of planting behind a shed in the garden, put one under your kitchen sink, by your office window. Watch it grow and water it, then use the mint in your iced tea, the basil on your sandwich, some thyme in your soup.

☐ **Dance, even if you're bad at it.** Dancing is like bacon—there's no bad version of it. It's all delicious. Because it's a feeling, in the moment, moving through you. Let go and get grooving. Everybody dance now.

☐ **Watch a kid swing up or slide down.** The next time you pass a park, stop and watch for a minute until you see a child in a moment of sheer glee, maybe sliding down a slide or kicking their little sneakers into the air on an upswing. It's a moment of sheer freedom and joy. *What can you do to feel the same?*

☐ **Bring greenery inside.** Buy yourself flowers. Or borrow from the earth, full of branches, blooms, and colorful leaves. Studies have found that gazing at greenery can help hospital patients heal faster, can lower crime, and can enhance creativity, as it symbolizes abundance and calm. Nature makes us happy, so use it!

☐ **Give your pillows a shake-up.** Turn your living room pillows backward and upside down. Un-lump them and re-fluff them. Then rotate them to different spots on the couch and chairs to give them—and you—a new view.

☐ **Belt it out in the shower.** Bellow a song loud and proud within your tile shower walls. The acoustics will make your voice shine—and maybe, with the windows open, make the neighbors smile.

☐ **Sleep under the stars.** In a tent, on a blanket; in a backyard or a clearing far away. Fall asleep with the night sky as your ceiling, the stars and moon your only light.

☐ **Observe new growth in the spring.** After a cold winter, a dry brush season, or a big storm, look for those tiny signs that life begins again: in the lively sprouts of evergreen branches, tiny buds of flowers, and palm fronds bursting toward the sky—all of them part of the cycle of life.

☐ **Eat a rainbow meal.** The more colors of food you have on your plate, the more varied the nutrients and vitamins you're getting for a balanced meal. Think: purple eggplant, yellow squash, red peppers, and green snow peas. Nibble a full plate of brightness.

☐ **Rock out when that cool part of the song breaks in.** You know that part—the one right after the bridge where the song is about to break loose and go bananas? Just as much as you love the song, you also love knowing that a key change or a beat breakdown is coming next. Appreciate the buildup, which is what makes the payoff so darn good.

☐ **Eat lunch in the fresh air.** Unpack your personal picnic on a bench, at a park table, on a front porch, or plopped down on a piece of grass. In the sun or shade, feel the fresh air on your face.

☐ **Get your blood moving for six minutes.** Do it with gusto and that's all it takes to get that refreshed, alive feeling that will help you ward off stress. That's because exercise releases the hormone norepinephrine, which helps the brain handle stress—thus, the less active we are, the more prone we are to depression and anxiety. So get that blood pumping and give your body the best chance to be happy.

☐ **Be your own hometown concierge.** If a tourist approached you in town, what would you recommend? To go window-shopping down the tree-lined avenues? To take a pedicab through the city streets? To order the local chowder at the best dive spot around? Take your own best advice, and visit the local sights with fresh eyes.

☐ **Try a new fruit or vegetable.** We get a weekly "farm box" delivery of seasonal vegetables and fruits from local farms. It's satisfying to have a fridge full of fresh food—but it's also fun being surprised by purple carrots and cactus fruit, and finding a clever way to use them. Whether you're cooking in or ordering out, challenge yourself to try new foods.

☐ **Have a cross-your-legs, pee-your-pants, wipe-your-eyes, hold-your-belly laugh.** It's good for you. The "Laughter Clubs" of India have the right idea: The muscular exertions involved in a solid laugh actually trigger the release of endorphins in the brain, known as the "feel good" chemicals. It also boosts virus- and cancer-fighting cells. So call that funny friend, watch that hilarious video, or think of what always makes you laugh and call it up when you need it.

☐ **Put a red lip on it.** I love this little tip I got from actress Addison Timlin, who was telling me her favorite way to amp up her mood instantly: "I put a red lip on it," she says. She may be wearing sweats and sneakers with her hair in a messy ponytail, but with a swipe of bright lipstick, she feels put together and cute. "A bold lip says, 'I'm here and I'm confident,'" says Addison, "'because if I weren't, do you really think I would draw this much attention to myself?'"

Get your own "red lip": Maybe it's your good watch, a bright shirt, a fab jacket, or just the right jewelry.

☐ **Move it outside.** The lunch meeting. The paperwork. The date. Sometimes we're the ones who box ourselves in, when there's a whole world out there to see. When the weather is spectacular, choose something from your regular inside routine and try it outside.

☐ **Celebrate a wee occasion.** Why save all the celebrations for holiday time, when everyone else is racing around, too? Toast to what means something special just to you: A pet's birthday. Your first date. One week of not smoking. The day it feels like you've officially broken in your shoes. Life offers little reasons for a party every single day.

☐ **Build a "Happy Box."** Fill a box, a basket, or a jar with things that make you smile. Add little notes on the positive things that happen to you, like "Someone on the bus complimented my coat." Include tickets to music shows that transported you, or funny photo booth pictures that make you laugh. When you need a reminder that good things are happening every day, your Happy Box is there to remind you.

☐ **Take it for a spin.** Test-drive the car. Try out the bike. Take the golf cart for a roll. Why not? It's a new view of the same world on a different set of wheels.

☐ **Go to sleep two hours earlier.** Whether it's a full eight hours or not, sleep is what gives us the energy to get up and live it up. So choose one night to dive under the covers crazy early—7 p.m., anyone? Find your sweet spot of snoozing happiness and give yourself a big leap on the day ahead.

☐ **Play with pattern.** Add some complex beauty to your life—with your clothes or in your home. Life offers too much for us to be dull! Be inspired by exotic prints from all over the world: Portuguese wall and floor tiles, motifs of trees and cherry blossoms from Japan, ikat-dyed textiles from Ecuador, swirls of henna designs from India, and colorful striped blankets in Mexico and Peru. Revel in multiple patterns of intricate splendor.

☐ **Take the leftovers challenge.** Make a week's worth of meals using only leftover items in your fridge and cupboards. Challenge yourself to dig deeper into the cupboards to complete each meal, turning mashed potatoes into a potato pancake and dicing the last of the veggies for an omelet. You'll feel resourceful, creative, economical, and probably full.

☐ **Pump some iron.** Recently, I found I practically needed a running start to get a revolving door moving, so I vowed to turn my stringy arms into strength; I'm still working on it. Join me: Do some push-ups. Lift some weights. Empower your upper body. Because your arms are symbolic for so many powerful things you do in life: lifting heavy things, pushing forward, holding on.

☐ **Create a spectrum.** Forget matchy-matchy. If you want to brighten the vibe in an instant, display one of every color you can think of. Put out a bright, bold collection of Post-it notes, paperclips, or pretty blooms. I even put the books with the most colorful spines at eye level on my bookshelf, which gives the room a truly happy feel.

☐ **Have a party for the full moon.** Instead of being surprised when you come across that big, bright orb in the sky, plan for it. How can you celebrate this month under a glowing moon? Lay a blanket out in the yard, plan a camping trip, or host your own "Full Moon Party" on a cold night with hot toddies and good friends.

☐ **Throw a "dart" finger on your local map and go there.** Add a dash of adventure to your routine. Hit a corner of the map, see what's there, and pop into the closest diner for a cup of joe in a different part of town.

☐ **Get crazy scared.** Being truly terrified isn't fun, but it can be invigorating to get scared in a safe place. It spikes your adrenaline, gets the blood pumping, and takes you out of your everyday mind-set. Watch a horror movie from the shelter of your living room or ride a roller coaster for a brief burst of hair-raising fun. It's good to jump out of your seat every once in a while.

☐ **Hit a local highlight.** The village museum. A local comedy show. The paint-your-own-pottery shop. Check it off your close-to-home bucket list for a little sense of escape at your doorstep.

☐ **Shout at the top of your lungs.** Belt out your wishes or your gratitude from a rooftop, the water's edge, or the car window on the highway. Scream whatever you want from the depths of your lungs and out into the big, wide world.

☐ **Use a spice you've never tried.** Variety is the spice of life, so give your spices some variety. I recently tried cooking with harissa, turmeric, and smoked paprika, which are now in my regular cooking rotation. Sample some of your own flavors from faraway cultures: Play with cardamom, cumin, saffron, or dried epazote. Challenge your taste buds and your creativity.

☐ **Take a different route home.** Head down a different block. And if you take the wrong exit, see it as an opportunity. There are even travel-inspired mobile apps (Dérive is one of them) that will chart a route to your destination by taking the long way or encouraging you to seek out interesting detours. Check out the buildings, the shrubbery, the people. They're probably much the same, just . . . different.

☐ **Run hot/cold.** When I was a kid at the town swimming pool, we loved hopping out of the water on a chilly day, taking a few freezing laps around it, then jumping back into the pool, which felt warmer than ever in comparison. Do this in your own way: Run the shower cold for a second to appreciate the hot, linger outside on a hot day before stepping into the air-conditioning, or touch your cold nose one last time before hopping inside to get warm.

☐ **Sneeze like you mean it.** A sneeze can be so satisfying if you let it do its job—ejecting particles that are irritating your nose at speeds from thirty-five miles an hour and more. So don't steal its thunder by nipping it in the bud! Give your next sneeze the opportunity of a good ol' "Ah-choooo!"

☐ **Eat something off the vine.** Pluck a grape off the vine. A blueberry off the bush. An apple from the tree. Or try some honeysuckle sap on the tip of your tongue.

☐ **Put something unusual on your toast.** Butter? Sure. But give your taste buds a different treat, too, just once. Try goat cheese, almond butter, passion fruit jam, or a soft avocado, smushed onto the surface with a splash of olive oil and salt.

☐ **Make a happy snap collage.** Some apps and computer programs can organize this for you, or you can make one yourself by hand: Take photos of ten things that make you happy—like a ceramic sculpture you love or your cat's little pink nose—and use them to decorate your computer desktop or fridge. Or collect your favorite photos in a collage file, and sift through them when you need a lift.

☐ **Wear the right bright thing.** A study out of the University of California on the effects of colors on emotions found that the greater the saturation and brightness of a color, the more arousing it is to our feelings. So choose a color that gives you a boost in whatever mood you need: a flash of green for freshness and growth; a pop of red for a powerful, confident punch; yellow for happiness and warmth; or a blue hue for a calming vibe.

☐ **Eat with your hands.** Have one fully finger-fed meal for fun: Eat your salad with your fingers. Your pasta. Your fried chicken or—if you're brave—your refried beans. Get in touch with your food, with no utensils to wash when you're done.

Be Thrilling

Share the gift of an experience. You can give your friend a bracelet for her birthday. Or you can give her an experience that enhances her life and provides her positive memories forever. According to research by Ryan Howell, PhD, happiness from material goods starts to fade between two and six weeks later, but the joy from an experience can last from months to a lifetime. Plus, new experiences elicit excitement, fear, nervousness, and glee—all things you can't wrap in a box.

- **Give someone a kick.** Send them hang gliding. Or off to a go-kart park. Or get them out fishing or whale-watching in a place they've never been.
- **Give someone an experience they'd never splurge on.** Like a gift certificate for a divine dinner, a spa visit, or a night at a rad hotel.
- **Give someone a chance to sample their interest.** Maybe it's a cocktail-making class, dancing lessons, or a horseback ride at sunset.

☐ **Learn to open a bottle in an unusual way.** Figure out how to pop open a beer or soda bottle with a lighter or table edge, or how to open a wine bottle with a rubber-soled shoe or—for the truly intrepid—a bike pump. Look these up; they're fun!

☐ **"Omakase" a meal.** In Japanese sushi, ordering *omakase* basically means, "I trust you," and allows the chef to select the meal for you, piece by piece. Let go and leave the choice up to someone else in your own life, sushi or otherwise: Let the chef or a friend order for you and sit back for a ride of small surprises.

☐ **Watch a dancer dance.** I'd been friends with my Colombian friend Jenn for twelve years before I finally saw her dance to Latin music—a booty-shaking and utterly fluid tour de force that was mesmerizing to watch. Stop and study a dancer, whether at the ballet or a subway station. Behold the human body as an instrument of grace.

☐ **Play closet roulette.** Pull out something you haven't worn in *ages* and work it into an outfit. You'll either find you forgot how much you loved it (score!) or that there's no reason to waste precious closet space with it a single day more.

☐ **Run for your life.** I'm not a marathon runner; well, nor am I a make-it-down-the-whole-block runner, either. But I know and appreciate the exhilarating feeling you get when you run or jump or climb to the point of being out of breath. Prove to yourself what your body can do.

Be Well

Make that appointment with the dentist. *Wait, huh?!* You may be thinking. *How is this supposed to make me happy?* Think about it like this: If you clean the dust off your refrigerator grille, it will keep your unit running efficiently and lengthen the life of your appliance. Well, the same goes for the appliance of *you*: Clean the dust off your teeth, too. (Or, maybe, it's time for a general physical, skin check, or blood work with the doctor.) Because true happiness isn't only about doing the *fun* things; it's about giving yourself the opportunity to have the fullest, biggest life. If you go today instead of next year, there will be less wrong, so it will hurt less, and it will cost less. In case this helps: Research shows if you visit the doc in the afternoon, your dental pain threshold will be at its highest. Be healthy. Be happy. Hey, silly: Go.

☐ **Get a flame going.** Earn yourself an imaginary Scouts badge by starting the flame in a campfire, a fireplace, a non-gas grill, or a bonfire on a beach. Whether you build a kindling tepee or use some tortilla chips as fire starters (they work, really!), you'll gain a flicker of pride when you get a spark going all on your own.

☐ **Eat for your whole body.** Be conscious of eating a sweet potato for the vitamin A for the health of your eyes, or eating kale for the vitamin K that helps your blood and bones. Really *feel* the food feeding you as it goes in. Challenge yourself to make a meal for your head to your toes, like wind running a mill, providing the nutrients each part of your body needs to keep the machine running.

☐ **Wear polka dots.** Be eccentric in your own way by wearing an item everyone *isn't* going to be wearing today. They may look twice, they may question your choice, or, like the way I felt when my friend Johnny White showed up in an orange velvet three-piece suit, they may wish they had the cojones to wear it, too. As actor David Arquette once told me in an interview, "I'd rather have a big fashion no-no than have no fashion style whatsoever." Borrow that boldness: Be brave and try something new.

☐ **Take it like they make it.** Sometimes we order the dressing on the side, the sandwich without the mayo, the sauce without the mushrooms, the burrito without the cheese. It's often for a healthy reason. But this time, get the meal as it comes. Enjoy the oozy or gooey or crunchy or cheesy goodness, just as its creator intended.

Be Perceptive

Do interval happiness check-ins. I have an experiment for you to try. Set a small alarm on your phone to go off every hour or so, ideally with a pleasant chirp sound more than the nuclear alarm one! When the alarm goes off, ask yourself: "Am I happy?" If the answer is yes, write what you're doing on the "happy" side of a checklist; if the answer is no, put it under the "not so much" column. At the end of the day, you'll have a little chart that might look like: **"What makes me happy:** Petting dog. Productive at work. Cold beer. Hug. **What makes me unhappy:** Stuck inside. Feeling lonely. Reading Internet. Stiff." Now, be the coach of your own team by rolling the video of your performance to gain some insight on what you might change if you could do an instant replay of the day. Maybe you cut down your time on the computer so you can connect with the people you love; or maybe you get outside more by taking your dog for an extra run. Use your check-ins to change your life.

☐ **Have an "out of body" day.** For one day, don't talk about your looks. That means you can't say, "I'm so fat" or "I feel ugly" or "I swear I've gained five pounds just looking at that pizza" or "What is *with* my hair?" No physical references. Your mind (and your friends) will thank you.

☐ **Yes, try a bite!** Your dining companion takes a bite, says, "Mmmm," and then asks, "Want a bite?" So what do you answer? Sometimes it seems too personal. Sometimes it seems like a hassle. But every time, it's worth it. So say yes and take a taste. Just a little one. Then put together a perfect little nibble in return. Let yourselves savor the different flavors as you connect through your taste buds.

☐ **Start a laugh journal.** When friends and I get laughing so hard it hurts, I write down what's funny on the list I keep on my iPhone's notepad. Then when I need a lift, I go back and read the quotes, reliving some of those belly laughs all over again. Create your own comical notebook: Write down what gets you going in a small notepad, a journal, or on your computer and keep the laughs coming.

☐ **Get popping.** I make a pot of 100 percent whole-grain, non-GMO popcorn a few times a week, spritzing it with olive oil spray and salt, or a shake of Old Bay seasoning or cayenne pepper. What's more fun than a snack food packed with antioxidants and fiber that transforms before your eyes from hard little kernels into crunchy balls of yum?

☐ **Try a sport you're certain you'd be terrible at.** Think of a sport you've never tried that you're guessing you'd stink at. Then . . . play it anyway! Swing at a golf ball, take a shot with a basketball, or try to break a rack at the pool table. You don't have to be any good to appreciate the fun of attempting it.

TWO

Wonder

Savor each second as you wake up your senses to the **brilliance** in the **present** moment. Seek out the small moments all around you that you may be missing. These vivid ideas will help you live more **mindfully**, with beautiful **awareness** of what you see, hear, taste, smell, and feel in the **now**.

☐ **Savor the very first bite of a delectable dish.** Close your eyes and make any sounds you want.

☐ **Wash your hands thoroughly.** Really scrub your hands, like a doctor prepping for surgery. Keep it up for at least twenty seconds, which is the time it takes to sing "Happy Birthday" twice. Wash off the grime, clean under your nails, and give your hands a fresh start. And as research out of the University of Michigan shows, if you suds up after making a tough decision—thus "washing your hands" of the struggle to make it—you are more likely to feel happy with your choice.

☐ **Scratch an itch.** We forget what a feat of joy it is to scratch where and when we need to, because we usually only feel it for a split second before our nails attack. Next time, note the itch so you can enjoy each small, satisfying second of scratching it away.

☐ **Give an airplane shout-out.** When you see an airplane fly directly overhead, spend a minute speculating on where it's headed. Picture one person on board as it heads off into the clouds. What are they doing? Where are they going? Who are they seeing? Maybe they're on their way to a wild safari or a tour of beautiful temples, or perhaps they're heading to visit their new grandchild for the first time. Even if we're not setting off on an epic journey, it's nice to think that someone is.

☐ **Don't run from the rain, run in the rain.** Rain is nature giving you a little shower. Hey, maybe it thinks you need it! So linger under the showerhead of the sky as it rinses you off for kicks. Relax and remember: It's only water.

☐ **Tune in to the steady noises in your neighborhood.** Church bells in the distance. Taxis honking. Lawn mowers cutting the grass. Delivery trucks opening their doors and dropping off their goods. Could you identify your neighborhood by sound alone?

☐ **Eat at half speed.** Be extremely mindful of what you're eating for a few forkfuls. Take one small bite. Rest. Then turn that taste into a slow, deliberate event.

☐ **Pick out the sounds of the birds.** In the right season or the right place, you can hear the birds chirp, but are you listening? For one minute, really tune in to their songs: Mockingbirds chirping. Robins peeping. Seagulls cawing. Learn the sounds of your local birds and enjoy the music they make. It's a concerto out there.

☐ **Carry a keychain you love.** You use it daily, so don't haul around something that's only so-so. Finding just the right bauble is the "key" to making you smile at every turn.

☐ **Find the Milky Way.** In a dark, dark sky, look for the Milky Way. This sign of the galaxy our solar system lives in, more than one hundred thousand light-years wide, full of more than two hundred billion stars. Sheesh, you can't count *that* on your fingers. Spend a few minutes in awe.

☐ **Squeeze the next hour dry.** There will never, ever be another hour like the one in front of you now. Think of the next sixty minutes as a soaked towel, and try to wring every drop out of it: Notice the diverse faces around you, and say yes to your instinct to make a turn, accept an opportunity, or stand still and just breathe the moment in.

☐ **Watch the movie in a reflection.** In a puddle, look for the reflection of clouds. On the shimmering chrome of a building, look for the reflection of the birds flying by. In a coffee shop window, see a sidewalk of people, bustling with life.

☐ **Make an echo.** Stand in the right spot under a curved ceiling and speak, or hoot into the arch of some rocks in a cave. Find a place where your voice can float off and bounce in an echo, singing that same song back to your ears.

☐ **Discover something beautiful in an old familiar place.** I was at a stoplight by my house—the one I'm at day after day—when I challenged myself to find something lovely I'd never seen before. And there it was: The tall trees were in perfect sets of two, lining the sidewalk. How had I never noticed before? Oh, right . . . I'd never *looked*. Find something newly beautiful in a spot you're in all the time.

☐ **Find a killer parking spot.** *Ooh*, you get to think as you pull straight in between the lines just steps from your destination, *now this was a good one.*

☐ **Walk barefoot on the grass.** Kick off your shoes, peel off your socks, and feel the blades beneath you. Fresh grass is a cushion for your soles, and a treat for your soul.

☐ **Enjoy the sound of food being made.** The eggs being cracked, the herbs being chopped, the churning of the food mixer. Listen as the dough is pounded in a pizza place, for the sizzle when food hits the oil in a hot pan.

☐ **Look out the airplane window.** That view you get from takeoff? You'd have to pay top dollar for that sight on an aerial tour from a small plane or helicopter. You're flying through the *air*, remember. Be that wide-eyed eager face pressed up against the window as you slip through the clouds and watch the scenery slide away.

☐ **Push through the brambles.** Enjoy the scratches from life's thorns as you head off the beaten path, every branch in your way a sign that you're braving new ground.

☐ **Stand in mountain pose.** Feel grounded by standing in *Tadasana*, or mountain pose, as you would in yoga. Stand with your feet together (big toes touching, heels apart), your shoulders back, your head straight up over your pelvis, and your arms down at your side, palms facing forward. Then close your eyes and breathe as you distribute your weight evenly on the "three arches" of your feet: your heel, your big toe, and your pinkie toe. Feel heavy, feel balanced, feel grounded. Feel one with the earth.

☐ **Open every window in the house.** Or just a window you've never opened. When I opened the far window in my office recently, a beautiful floral scent floated in. Give yourself a new breeze, new light, new aromas.

☐ **Listen to a child learning.** Whether it's your child talking or a kid in the ice cream shop, you are witnessing the astonishing sound of a small human learning how to get by in life: how to open a box, play a game, figure out the world, and find their way.

☐ **Flip through a travel magazine or site.** You may not be able to visit the places you see, but it's a beautiful reminder of all the earth has to offer—from mountains to beaches to modern cities. Transport yourself there with your mind.

☐ **Enjoy a TV-free day.** For twenty-four hours, don't touch that remote (or your computer if that's how you're watching your shows). Enjoy the silence of a room without an announcer or a laugh track and fill your time with other things: Play cards, read a book, start a stew, sit outside with a coffee. It's like pressing the "Restore" button on life, bringing you back to the basics.

☐ **Take a tour of bug land.** When I picked up a flowerpot in my backyard recently, an entire world of creatures came crawling to life: wiggly worms and balled-up bugs scurrying into life. What a huge community I'd never thought about before. Squat down, take a look, have a little visit.

☐ **Breathe in a bakery.** Wow, a whole store devoted to baking things that make us happy: muffins, bread, croissants, cupcakes, cookies, and pastries dotted with fruits and frosting. What good people they are, rolling dough, adding sugar, tempering chocolate, and popping it all in the oven for us. Whether you eat any of it or not, delight in the scrumptious scent.

☐ **Follow a wave or ripple.** When we get a chance to see waves or a ripple of water from a tossed stone's throw, we often take in the big picture of them all: the waves, the ripples. This time, follow just *one* with your eyes. Take it from start to finish, the full cycle of energy on a journey.

☐ **Sing along to the store soundtrack.** It's always such a surprising pleasure when a song you love starts playing

---

Feel Awe

Get your "awe" on for two minutes. A study from Stanford University found that an awe-inspiring experience can make us happier and nicer—perhaps, they say, because it feels like time has slowed down and we have far more of it to spare. Thus, *ahhhh*. The earth is a canvas for nature's art, so open your eyes to life's great gallery. Let yourself be awed. There is enough here to blow us away every single day.

- **Seek awe in the sea.** Catch dolphins leaping through the sea or birds diving for their dinner.
- **Seek awe in the sky.** Sit in lawn chairs for a sunrise or watch some immense storm clouds roll in.
- **Seek awe in the ground.** Observe a succulent flowering with vibrant colors, or a fruit tree in full bloom.
- **Seek awe in the heavens.** Revel in the grand majesty of outer space, or see the moon through a telescope up close.

---

when you're away from home. Appreciate that moment, when someone else seems to be DJing to your distinctive tastes. Sing along or get a lift in your step as if the party in aisle ten is meant for you.

☐ **Travel afar.** Let's be honest: Your schedule will never be wide open, your bank account never flush enough. But you still deserve an adventure. Don't wait until you're older. Find a way to book a trip that takes your breath away now.

☐ **Be all skin-feely.** We're used to the idea of trying to "be happy in your own skin," but how often do we really *feel* ourselves in our own skin? It's our largest organ—we adults have over twenty square feet of it!—packed with sensory receptors. Feel the breeze against your arms and cheeks. Notice your skin against your pants, your socks, your shoes, and your back against the spine of the chair.

☐ **Witness true balance.** If you study the shapes of a few trees, you'll notice that while the sides may not be evenly filled, together each one is in balance as a whole. Learn from the trees, prudently filling in one area to balance what you may lack in another. Nature knows how to do this. We can, too.

☐ **Sleep on a new side of the bed.** Get out of that little rut you've made in the mattress and try the other side. Even if you and a partner have been sharing for years, mix it up and see what it feels like to wake up with a brand-new view.

☐ **Appreciate the details.** La Sagrada Familia church in Barcelona, Spain, designed by Antoni Gaudi, has been under construction since 1882. Why is it taking so long to complete? Well, because the beauty of the design lies, literally, in the small, striking details. It makes me think about how many little features we may miss that someone else has worked so hard to make. Look for them today: The carvings over an old wooden door. The tiling of a path through the park. The sugar design on top of a cupcake. Enjoy them the way their makers dreamed we would.

☐ **Get your hands dirty.** Plant a vegetable garden, repot a window plant, or help a friend weed a flower bed. Push your hands deep down into the soil and connect yourself with the earth.

☐ **Listen for the sounds the wind creates.** Leaves rustling down a sidewalk. Weather vanes squeaking. House walls rattling. Air whistling through a crack in a window.

☐ **Read a book about happiness to remind you what really matters.** Oh look, you already did! As the Brits say, good on ya. Go ahead and check this item off.

☐ **Watch a bird in flight for as long as you can.** Marvel in how it flaps its wings, how it dips and soars, how it seems

---

Be Grateful

Try the "Grateful in Four Seconds" practice. The more senses involved in a task, the more it impacts our memory— which is why when you're learning a language, it's good to hear it *and* speak it, or hear it *and* read it. Using that same idea, give as many senses to your *gratitude* that you can. Look around the room, find what you're grateful for, then touch it and offer four seconds of a focused, full-on thank-you out loud. You will see that you're surrounded by things that have added to your life: lamps that bring light, art that brings beauty, and family that brings love.

- **Touch the orchid** on your coffee table and say, "I'm grateful you provide life and brightness to some dreary days."
- **Touch your dear friend's shoulder** and say, "I'm grateful you always make me feel supported."
- **Touch your comfiest chair** and say, "I'm grateful I have a snug place to settle in after a long day."
- **Touch your pet** and say, "I'm grateful you provide affection when I need it."

---

to sit, sometimes, on a gust of wind. Nature has given us all gifts. The birds get to move through the air above us, and we're the ones who get to contemplate the miracle.

☐ **Applaud great feats of engineering.** Before that bridge you know was built, it was a swath of space or water, separating lands. Before that tunnel was burrowed, it was a wall of rock or a sheet of water. It's so easy to take advancements like these for granted. So today, notice the profound feats of engineering by hardworking human beings—from skyscrapers to dams to machinery that helps us get things

---

Do New

Do the new version. To give yourself a fresh perspective, try doing as many new things as possible.

- **Eat a new breakfast.** If you always have a banana and oatmeal, try kiwi and almonds in yogurt. Shock your system with a surprise in the first hours of the day.
- **Move things around on your desk.** Switch the lamp to the other side. Change the items on your bulletin board.
- **Walk to the bank instead of driving.** Or ride a bike instead of walking. Change how you get to your usual locations and you'll feel like you're experiencing something for the very first time.

done. Write a mental thank-you note for these gifts from our predecessors, a moment of respect for all they made.

☐ **Behold the show of the sunset.** It happens every night . . . but just a little bit differently for every spot we stand upon the earth. It's a small reminder that we're spinning, in the universe, bidding good night to the sun while we rest.

☐ **Appreciate an outdoor scent.** The fragrance of grass being mowed. A neighbor using their fireplace. The scent of pine trees lining a path. The first few seconds of fresh rain on a street.

☐ **Snuggle into a toasty moment.** When you step in from the cold to defrost in the warmth of your living room or when you climb into a car that's been warming up on a winter morning! Feel yourself melt as the heat thaws you out, body and soul.

☐ **Sniff out the familiar scents in your home.** We all have a different default scent in our homes, depending on what we do most. Notice what's building yours: Garlic sautéing on the stove. The cleaner you used to wipe down the counter in the kitchen. Fresh laundry. Perfume spritzing. Baby baths. Brownies baking in the oven. Breathe in the fragrance that makes your space become your home.

☐ **Choose your seat wisely.** I once had an awe-inducing flight with a seat facing the sunset for three hours. Maybe you can book your next plane seat so you can catch dawn, or see a country's coast, or get a good view of the Rockies. You can also do this with your morning commute: Pick a seat on the bus or train that lets you watch the sights, or drive yourself down the road that has the most rewarding landscape.

☐ **Bring someone to their "first."** Their first lobster. Their first meditation class. Their first screening of a film by a director you admire. If you find yourself feeling accustomed to something you've tried or seen many times, experience someone else's first to reignite how special it is for you. *Mmmm*, you'll remember. *I forgot how good this was.*

☐ **Enjoy some old-fashioned sounds.** We hear enough of our cell phones ringing and computer keys tapping. But we're also still gifted with the sounds of a time gone by, too: A grandfather clock ticking in the hall. The hum of a fan. The crackle of a fire. The purr of an old egg timer. A heater clacking or hissing as it warms up a room.

Be Mindful

Be in the now, one minute at a time. Make it a regular practice to try what's known as "mindfulness"—keeping a focused attention on the present, from your breath to your thoughts to your body sensations. It's good for more than your soul. According to research out of the Mindful Awareness Research Center at UCLA, mindful meditation can combat unhealthy inflammation in the body and can increase the body's enzyme telomerase, which slows down aging. So give your mind and body a gift and be present.

- **Be a mindful eater.** Pay attention to your food, from when you see it to when you swallow. Enjoy the colors and the shapes. Note the aroma wafting to your nose. Then take a small bite, feeling the textures, and savoring the flavors on your tongue.
- **Be a mindful walker.** Feel your muscles working in unison as you take a step, setting down your front foot and pushing off the back. You are balanced and grounded and strong.
- **Be a mindful meditator.** You don't need to be a Zen master. Just try ten minutes of sitting in silence. Feel your breath moving in and out, your chest rising up and down, your nerves calming. When you feel under control, so will life.

☐ **Take in the zoo around you.** We'll travel to view animals in enclosures, but what about the zoo of animals at our feet every day? There are deer and rabbits in the suburbs; squirrels and pigeons in the city; maybe a cat or dog on your lap right now. Celebrate the wildlife we get to have at home.

☐ **Look into a baby's eyes.** Those fresh eyes taking in every blink and smile and move in this new world.

☐ **Thank your hands.** They've been with you your whole life—holding, touching, carrying, typing, writing, wringing, clapping, praying. If one or both are with you still, caress them and be kind to them for all they've done.

THREE

Comfort

It's important for human beings to feel secure and **safe**, to have that **cozy** feet-up-on-the-coffee-table-at-**home** feeling. Cuddle up with these **soothing** ideas of **self-care**, like a **warm** blanket, for a natural, fruitful life.

☐ **Make(over) your bed.** When it comes to sleep, your bed is meant to help you rest and recharge, so help it help you: Update your duvet, put on softer sheets, add a blanket. Swaddle yourself in comfort when you need it most.

☐ **Make a soup with what you've got.** Sauté onions in olive oil. Add carrots or celery or other vegetables from the fridge. Pour in water or stock. Adds beans or herbs. Give your body something nourishing, satisfying, simple, and good.

☐ **Get a pair of "comfy pants."** Whether you change into yoga pants, "sleepy pants," sweats, or pj's, cozy clothes signal a shift in your day from your public "I dressed for you all" look to a laid-back "Who cares, I'm comfortable!" one.

☐ **Super stock up on that thing you keep running out of.** Like coffee, toilet paper, pet food, or salt. My home is always so short of toothpaste, I grabbed ten tubes at a recent sale and now brush with delight, knowing I'm not using the last of it every time. In the same way, treat yourself to the little luxury of having more than enough of what you need.

☐ **Drink a cup of hot cocoa.** What do you get when you cross a hot mug, a rich drink, and melting marshmallows? The feeling that you're taken care of. And as research continues to show, even a little bit of real dark chocolate can boost your mood.

☐ **Make a "Happy Wall."** We'll often fill a wall space with something—*anything*—so it's not empty. Today, update one of your walls with only what brings you joy. With art you adore. Framed family photos. A mirror you decorated yourself. Or a shelf filled with driftwood you collected with your kids. Choose whatever feeds your spirit so you can gaze at it in one place every day.

☐ **Live in your beautiful mess.** That's right, a day full of mess can be beautiful, too, because it's *your* mess: dishes dirtied with a good meal, comforters crumpled from a long sleep, and sneakers in the hall after a day of family fun. This one time, don't stress about cleaning up. Your as-is mess is all yours.

☐ **Ask yourself, "If I moved today, what would I miss the most?"** Maybe it's a secret path in the park. The view from your roof deck. Your favorite local Thai place. You don't need to be on the go to go appreciate it as soon as you can.

☐ **Sleep in.** Arrange for a morning with no reason or nudge to get up at all: No alarm clock buzzing. No baby crying. No phone ringing. No texts dinging. Hire a sitter or take a day off if that's what you need for a lingering, uninterrupted lie-in. Just you and your dreams, as long as you need.

☐ **Play an album you haven't listened to in twenty years.** When you hear a comforting old song on the radio, it transports you back to a time when life was less complicated. So consciously send youself on that simple music journey: Dig up a song you once loved from the music in your closet or a playlist online and turn up the volume to the good memories of your past.

☐ **Plant something purely for the scent of it.** A jasmine vine, a mint plant, some lavender for the window box. Rather than the sight of it, plant it for the smell.

☐ **Say "ahhhh" when you put your head on your pillow.** That familiar treadmill of routine—wake, eat, work, sleep, repeat—can make us forget that after a big, long day or a vacation away, it is such a safe, soothing few seconds when you lay down your head into a cloud of comfort. Exhale, relax, and say "ahhhh."

☐ **Pour the first drops from a full, fresh pot.** Whether you're pouring a fresh pot of coffee into an empty mug or a full pitcher of homemade lemonade into a chilled glass, it's blissful to tilt and dispense that first delicious serving.

☐ **Treat your feet.** Put an extra soft rug along the edge of your bed so the first thing your bare feet feel in the morning is plushness. Or try one in another surprising spot. I put a thick rug at the foot of my washer and dryer so I can fold and stack in a little luxury, with a safe, clean spot for socks to fall.

☐ **Watch someone sleep.** A cat curled up in the sun. A baby in a crib. A partner you love. Borrow the energy of their serene sleep and take a moment of quiet for yourself.

☐ **Snap your happy-at-home memories.** When you're on a trip, you shoot a week's worth of happy memories, right? So why not build a collection from what you see daily? Take photographs of your favorite moments at home: your morning teacup, your olive oils on a shelf, the pizza box on the floor while you watch the big game on TV. Your every day is as beautiful as the far away.

☐ **Have a pajama party for one.** Wear your coziest pajamas longer than you need. Put them on for dinner. Or spend a whole day wearing them, from dawn until dusk.

☐ **Make a cave.** On a sunny day, draw the blinds in your bedroom. Or darken your living room for movie time. Or build a fort with a blanket over the backs of chairs and curl up to read inside. It doesn't have to be a rainy day to hole up in the comfort of darkness.

☐ **Get your scalp rubbed.** Close your eyes and enjoy it at the shampoo bowl when you're getting a haircut. Ask for it to be added to your massage. Trade head rubs with your mate. Or use a scalp massager to give it a tingle yourself.

☐ **Name a plant, then care for her.** I have a friend with a "brown thumb" who swears she can't keep anything in a pot alive. So I gave her a new plant and told her this: "Name her." She made her plant a friend that needed caring for, and now she's more conscious about when her friend gets thirsty, so she feeds her. Give your plants a full life, too.

☐ **Bake bread.** It is astounding to see with your own eyes how flour, water, yeast, and salt can turn from ingredients in your pantry into a heap of sustenance. And nothing does your home better than the scent of baking bread, like a cartoon whiff of heaven. Work some dough with your bare hands and you'll appreciate all good bread to come.

☐ **Dive into your emotion.** Sometimes when we're sad, we fight back—by watching an uplifting comedy or seeing happy friends. This time, dive deeper into the well of your feelings. If you're sad, get sadder; choose a movie that will make you sob neck-wetting tears. It feels good to *feel*. And more important, it allows you to move on.

☐ **Warm up.** Warm your towel on a heater while you shower. Put on your pants right out of the hot dryer. Take a warm shower, or sit in a steam room or sauna, which science says can lift your mood. According to research, sensations of warmth affect the "happiness" neurotransmitters in the brain, serotonin. Even a mug of steaming mint tea can be a mood lifter. So turn up the heat.

☐ **Redefine what you see as "art."** We're the curators of our own lives, of what we choose to surround ourselves with. My fashion-forward friend Yvonne, for instance, displays her favorite couture shoes on a shelf. So display what you love: Maybe it's a collection of vintage pins or a friend's sketch on the back of an office memo. If it's beautiful to you, put it up, proud.

☐ **Get an extra thingie.** Grab an extra charger so that you have one at home *and* one at work. Pack an extra camera battery so you can charge one while you use one. Or pick up an extra bottle of eye drops so you can keep one in your bathroom cabinet *and* toss one in your bag. Relax, sit back, and use the extra within arm's reach.

☐ **Concentrate warmly on an old friend.** Have you ever thought about someone you miss, then run into them within hours or days? Call on that higher universal power that brings us together: Create an intention of who you'd love to run into, and you just may see them on the street soon, saying, "It's so weird, I was *just* thinking about you . . ."

☐ **Fix an item you love instead of replacing it.** Don't give up on those beloved jeans. They can be saved! Sew up the knee rip, re-hem those frays, and have a new zipper installed. They've spent years forming to your body, and you'll appreciate them even more for having survived.

☐ **Scent your home to the season.** In August, my house smells like magnolia blossoms; in December, like a festive cider of orange and cloves. Whether you light scented candles or carry in evergreen boughs, when the seasons change outside, celebrate through new scents inside.

☐ **Cozy up a floor space.** Layer a smaller rug onto wall-to-wall carpet or add some floor pillows and a blanket around the TV to build a conversation pit. Make the floor as fun to be on as any other spot in the house.

☐ **Ask, "Am I most at ease in this?"** It's easy to be influenced by current styles—but trends mean nothing if they're not bringing out the best of you. So the next time you get dressed, picture yourself entering the room: Will you feel at ease? Could you glow all day in what you're wearing? True beauty and confidence comes when you feel dressed like your best *you*.

☐ **Do something small for your safety out there.** Fill the oil in your car. Check the air pressure in your bike tires. Wear a reflective vest for walks at night. Be as safe out in the world as you are at home.

☐ **Find a book you can't bear to put down.** Choose a book you want to snuggle up with and get lost in for hours. Maybe it's a classic or maybe it's a pulpy, thrilling read. Highbrow or lowbrow, from the local library or a teenager's shelf, pick one you can't wait to open and are crushed to put down.

☐ **If it's beautiful, find a way to use it.** If you found a small piece of fabric you love at a small market in Italy, frame it as art on your bedroom wall. If you're drawn to a hand-painted cup you stumbled upon at a thrift store, turn it into a desk holder for your pens. If it speaks to you, find a way to display it. Reinvention will make it even more yours.

☐ **Accept the add-on massage.** You know that five-minute shoulder massage they offer at the pedicure place, the airport, or the shoe-shine spot? Take it. Five minutes can feel longer than you think when you're being rubbed into a relaxed little noodle.

☐ **Ask for a sign.** Life likes to give them to us. Or maybe we're just seeing what we want to in life. Either way, if you ask with your heart and pay attention with your soul, you'll get a reassuring clue in the right direction.

☐ **Create a new favorite craving.** Want to like the taste of something that, so far, you really don't? You can. A 2010 study found that repeated tasting of almost any food brings a familiarity and love for it. If you wish you loved olives, beets, dill, cilantro, or whatever else the rest of the world seems to appreciate, you can learn to crave the flavor, too. So eat and repeat until you do!

☐ **Appreciate an everyday feat.** Give yourself a "good job" nod when you slide into a parallel parking spot on the first

---

Get Perspective

Make your problems seem instantly small. Boy, we human beings are resilient. Not only do setbacks sometimes make us stronger, wiser, and happier, but later, we often can't even remember feeling the pain. The key, really, is getting through it in the *now*. Instead of being overwhelmed by a big issue, try to look at it from a new perspective. Here are two ways that can help:

- **Think about last year's "today."** Imagine yourself sitting back in a rocking chair on the front porch in one year or twenty and thinking back on this particular difficulty. Will it be behind you? Will it have worked itself out? The problem that seems enormous today may be barely a memory as time goes on.
- **Visit a spot where you can see the grandness of earth.** Catch a view of the vast sea, of a large meadow filled with wildflowers, of rooftops spreading out across a big city. You may be able to see your issue as one more thing that can be tackled in the grand scheme of a great life.

---

try. Or when you've applied a mailing label perfectly straight. Or when the container you choose to pour your leftovers into turns out to be *exactly* the right size. Oh, the simple satisfaction of getting it right.

☐ **Have breakfast in bed.** Make this the month you dine under your duvet. It's just so luscious, so over-the-top posh. The eggs and toast on a tray, propped up with a pillow. You deserve it.

☐ **Step into history.** What's the oldest spot in town? Is it a church, a restaurant, a museum, or a barbershop? Pay it a visit and notice the details: Maybe it's a well-worn hard-wood floor; timeworn shelves that have stocked items for decades; walls full of nicks and cracks from stories past; or photographs of what life was once like here. It's proof that while everything changes, pieces of the past remain.

☐ **Settle in for a show you've been looking forward to.** Find a perfect spot on the couch, cover your legs with just the right throw, and arrange a snack and a drink at your side. And as you raise your hand to turn on your television or radio program, feel that electricity—your anticipation of pressing Play and escaping into another world.

☐ **Put a happy photograph in an uncommon place.** Hang it in the garage by your yard tools, in the basement by the washer, or in the bathroom beside the sink. Choose a photo

---

Find Bliss

Come up with your "Instant Happy" formula. One Saturday morning, I was reading in bed when I realized my formula for happiness at that moment was just so simple: "Coffee, cat, book, bed, happy." A few days later, munching on my snack at the movie theater, I thought, "Popcorn, movie, soda, rom-com, happy." What are your formulas for happiness? Find a few. Maybe: "**Child**, bicycle, ice cream, giggles, happy." "**Beer**, football, burger, friends, happy." "**Date**, wine, mac and cheese, happy." In addition to the scenes that involve the people you love, also choose one that *doesn't* require other people to get it done. Yes, your baby, boyfriend, or best friend can make you happy. But kids wail, partners argue, and friends can disappoint you. So in those cases, you should have a mantra for just you. Think: "**Music**, walk, dog, neighborhood, happy." "**Garden**, water, soil, sunshine, happy." "**Sneakers**, running, breeze, park, happy." It's simple life math. What adds up to bliss for you?

---

representing the relationships that ground you or what gives your life its flavor—and let it remind you when you least expect it.

☐ **Appraise your bed pillows.** Life's too short to sleep on lumpy, droopy, stiff, bad pillows. So if you don't love *all* the pillows on your bed, edit. Make sure your head is happy snuggling into them all.

☐ **Add soft lighting to a surprising place.** My decorator friend inspired me with this one when I saw an elegant lamp on her modern kitchen countertop. Now when I entertain in the backyard on summer evenings, I put small table lamps on the outside picnic table, which I hope makes guests feel right at home. Switch it up yourself: Move a floor lamp from one corner of the room to another or add a gorgeous little glow to a dining hutch, a bathroom nook, or your office space.

☐ **Do something small for your safety at home.** Buy a fresh fire extinguisher. Fix the lock on your back door. Put flashlights and candles in arm's reach. Be prepared so you can sit back and rest indoors with ease.

Be Accepting

Take the compliment. Sometimes accepting a compliment is like letting a fly land on your leg and leaving it there when we want so badly to bat it away! Instead, try receiving what they're saying with grace.

- **Simply say "thank you."** If someone likes your shirt or shoes or hair, don't argue. Say "thanks."
- **Take the credit.** If you led a team to success, don't pass off the credit to everyone but yourself. Humble is nice, but dang it, you deserve to feel proud, too.
- **Stop discount divulging.** Contrary to a common female custom, if you get a compliment on your dress, you are not contractually obligated to reveal that you "got it for, like, twenty bucks." Likewise, you don't have to admit the diamonds on your jewelry are fake, the platinum is plated, and the cashmere . . . well, isn't. Just once, keep your secret to yourself.

☐ **Unplug an appliance you don't use every day.** The blender, maybe; the toaster, the printer. Yes, you'll have to plug it in again before you use it, but think about it: You don't have the iron plugged in and ready to go every minute, do you? Lighten the hum around you and give the planet a little break, too.

☐ **Give your space an upgrade.** What if your juice cup was made of nice china? If your bathroom towels were stocked in a wooden armoire? If your desk was a butcher-block kitchen table? Don't save the beautiful things for one spot or two; make the items in all your rooms your favorites.

☐ **Bring tranquility to your bedroom.** Remove: a television, a computer monitor, or a box of old shoes stuffed under the bed. Add a soft paint color to the walls, a framed painting that calms you, or a blanket that warms you. Make your bedroom a sanctuary of serenity.

☐ **Wear down your slippers.** Even better than a new pair of slippers or around-the-house shoes are a pair that wear right along with you—the padding molding around your arches, the soles waning beneath your toes. Put those babies on another pair of feet and it would go all wrong, right? These are *yours*.

☐ **Freshen up what's on your fridge.** Overhaul the hub of your house by switching up what's on your fridge. Clean off what's been there for years, then pin it full of different postcards, photographs, drawings, lists, or memories. Give yourself a new view as you reach for your fresh food.

☐ **Get a grown-up blankie.** As a kid, my soft piece of warmth was a square piece of turquoise yarn, crocheted by my aunt Joan. Now, I have a new one: an oatmeal-colored cashmere throw my mother gave me, and I cuddle under it in bliss almost every day. Make sure you have a cozy blankie of your own, to tuck your cold toes under on a chilly night.

FOUR

Delight

The more you **smile**, the more happiness you'll feel at your core. These **fun** ideas can keep you from taking life too seriously. Bring out the goofy **kid** in your heart, the **silly** lightness in your soul, and the **laughs** from your belly.

☐ **If someone offers you a crayon, use it.** Maybe it's a child with construction paper on the floor. Maybe it's a restaurant with white paper on the dining tables. Take the crayon. Then doodle, draw, and color outside your own lines.

☐ **Eat straight from the cake.** No plate, no spatula, no manners . . . and maybe just a little mess.

☐ **Rearrange a room.** Move the couch or push the bed against a different wall. Rustle the stagnant energy, refresh yourself—and vacuum under the nightstand that hasn't moved in years. Clean, fresh, and new, for just the cost of your energy.

☐ **Hold a balloon.** What a perfect emblem of lightness. A round balloon full of nothing but air. For lifting, floating, celebrating.

☐ **Feed an animal a treat.** Give a dog a bone. A duck some bread. A squirrel some nuts. Enjoy their lack of table manners as they dive right in.

☐ **Get a pair of "funglasses."** You probably already have a pair of sunglasses that flatter your face or look pretty cool, but consider adding a pair of funglasses to your collection that are just for goofy show. My current funglasses are black with little white polka dots, while another pair have square apricot-colored frames. Trust me: They're guaranteed to make others grin and make your photos more fun.

☐ **Drive with all the windows open.** Sure, your hair will get messed up, but who cares? It's liberating to let the fresh air fly around you however it feels like.

☐ **Figure out a trick you can do with your toes.** Pick up a pencil? Do a little dance? Grasp a spoon? Whether you can do any of those or none, it's worth the laugh trying to find out.

☐ **Have breakfast for dinner.** Or dinner for breakfast. Or pumpkin pie for lunch. Or—my very favorite—a bucket of movie popcorn for dinner. Make a menu in your own time.

☐ **Play some island music.** Play a Hawaiian song, with the strums of a ukulele, or a song from the Caribbean, packed with happy pats of steel drums.

☐ **Set a special occasion table on a weeknight.** Add a tablecloth, candlelight, a centerpiece maybe. Make it on a Wednesday night, for one or two, or your whole family. And if someone asks, "What's the occasion?" answer, "We are."

☐ **Do something "superfast" or "superslow."** I used to be able to play the Dolly Parton song "9 to 5" on the guitar, super fast. And my friend Phillip does an amazing dance in super-slow-motion for laughs. Flip real time on its head and see how fast you can cook, or how slow you can bowl—which kinda makes you appreciate when things take just as long as they need.

☐ **Make a paper plane that flies.** Double fold the wings for a super skinny glider or fold flaps for some stunts. Sneak a peek at the simple designs at 10paperairplanes.com—I'm all about the cool design called "The Moth"—and see what flies best for you.

☐ **Get a happy hat.** "Oh, hats don't look good on me," you might think. Yes, they do. The right one does. Hit a hat shop, try some on, have a chuckle, and wear one to declare a happy mood.

☐ **Take a well-considered picture.** Spend a minute longer than you normally might to frame the best shot you can. Aim it at the garden and ask, what, really, is the best composition? Maybe from an angle more left or right, the

---

Be a Kid Again

Do something that will make you go "Wheee!" Who said kids get to have all the fun? Regularly embrace what brings a little "yippee" into your life. Play like you used to.

- **Swing.** Climb onto a swing at the school park, or leap from a rope swing over a lake. Feel the freedom of letting go and making your stomach flip.
- **Ride.** Ride the Ferris wheel. Ride a horse. Ride a camel or a dune buggy on the sand.
- **Play.** Play one-on-one basketball or a game of tag. Take a swing with the bat or a kick at the ball and get yourself in the game.
- **Jump.** Off a bench. A diving board. A sand dune. Leap and feel the lightness all the way down.

---

camera raised above your head or on the grass from an ant's point of view. What a satisfying feeling when a small change can make it even better.

☐ **Whack something.** A baseball with a bat. A tennis ball with a racquet. A mole in a carnival game with a mallet.

☐ **If they're giving away lollipops, take one.** Banks often have them, a real estate office, maybe. But instead of putting it in your purse or pocket, open it right then—even if you only get a few fun licks out of it.

☐ **Try to sing an instrumental song.** Make your voice do its best to mimic the instruments from a classical song, a TV show intro, or synthesized dance music (I dare you to try Enya). It'll either sound badass or hilariously bad.

☐ **Go barefoot in an odd place.** Kick off your shoes on the rock jetty. The marble piazza. The mossy forest floor. This time you'll grin while you "bare" it.

THE HAPPY LIFE CHECKLIST

☐ **Have your favorite "birthday kid meal."** My parents used to let us kids pick our favorite meal to eat on our birthday. Think of what you might have chosen as a child: Was it meatloaf, fried rice, chicken nuggets, or something on the grill? Treat yourself today to your favorite kid meal.

☐ **Create your own touchdown dance.** In American football, players who score a touchdown spend about four to eight seconds celebrating in their own unique way— hopping, waving, jumping, and more. So come up with a crazy way you can ham it up the next time you succeed.

☐ **Say, "Yes, and . . ."** One of the rules of improv comedy is that when one comic throws out a funny line or a silly scenario, their fellow comics never say no or reject the idea. Instead, they think, "Yes, and . . ." They go with it, by adding something *else* fun to the pot. Do the same today. Just say yes and . . . let life surprise you with what it brings.

☐ **Leap through a sprinkler.** Or hop near a fountain, close enough to feel the spritz.

☐ **Learn one good, clean joke.** Choose one you can use for any occasion or audience. If you want, borrow one of these: (1) Two radio antennas met on a roof, fell madly in love, and decided to get married. The ceremony was just okay but the reception was excellent. (2) There was a man who entered a pun contest in his local paper. He sent in ten different puns, hoping at least one might win. Unfortunately, no pun in ten did. And (3) What did the 0 say to the 8? "Nice belt."

☐ **Drink a cold, fresh, fizzy soda.** Sugary or just seltzer-y; citrusy, bright, or tart, just soak up that perfect first sip.

☐ **Play the most joyful song ever.** It's good for your soul *and* heart. Researchers at the University of Maryland found that when participants listened to a joyful song, their blood vessels dilated by 26 percent, increasing cardiovascular health. So play a dance song you love, a gospel track like "Oh Happy Day," or some doo-wop if it makes you smile. Bring joy to your heart, literally.

☐ **Have a glass of wine or a cup of tea in a surprising place.** Have a French rosé in the bath or shower. Or sip a

> ## Be Grateful
>
> **Do a weekly gratitude roundup of "Five Good Things."** We often end our day by watching the news or stressing over something we wish we hadn't said. But don't sleep on it if it's a *bad* "it." Let yourself rest easy by taking a moment to go over the good stuff. In the 2003 study "Counting Blessings Versus Burdens," psychology researchers Robert Emmons and Michael McCullough found that acknowledging the good stuff—literally counting one's blessings—led to higher levels of well-being, physically and emotionally. To put it simply, "Gratitude is the antidote to negative emotions," writes Sonja Lyubomirsky, PhD, a prominent researcher in positive psychology. So, once a week—maybe every Saturday night or Monday morning—make a mental list of the five things you're most grateful for. Start with, "This week I am grateful for _____." Maybe it's your health, your new phone, the sunlight in the kitchen, or the family trip that brought you closer. Big and small, thank it all.

hot tea or a latte on a raft in a pool. Drink up the feeling of doing it a little upside down.

☐ **Do a cartwheel.** If your body will allow it, give it a try. You don't need good form to feel the thrill of twisting like a windmill off your arms through the air.

☐ **Overdress for the heck of it.** My friends from London introduced me to the idea of holding "Fancy Dress Nights," when we'd put on our nicest frocks and hit the town. Have your own: Put a tie on when you're not required, or a dress when slacks will do; or add some sequins, or super-high heels. Ditch the fear of being overdressed and wear your fancy duds with confidence.

☐ **Play fetch.** Grab a ball or Frisbee and toss it to a four-legged friend. Lap up their tail-wagging, tongue-panting, legs-churning joy, and let it get you thinking about what brings *you* that kind of glee.

☐ **Open a book to your "mantra" for the day.** Open a book, magazine, or catalog, close your eyes, turn to a random page, and point. Then, open your eyes to see what sentence you've landed on, and try to use the idea as a fun theme for the day. A sentence about ancient times? Reflect on your ancestors. One about climbing aboard a boat? Imagine how you can set off for an hour and feel that free.

☐ **Sniff a happy scent from childhood.** Play-Doh. Baby wipes. Crayola crayons. Coconut sunscreen. Candy. Why?

Because our sense of smell is intimately linked to the brain's limbic system—the same area where our emotions are born and our emotional memories are stored. So the slightest scent can send us reeling back in time, reconnecting us with sweet memories of simpler days.

☐ **Cash in your coins.** My husband and I like to redeem our jar of collected coins before every vacation and use the newfound money to buy ourselves a treat—like a pair of foot massages or an extra night at a nice hotel. See what little (or big) splurge your coins can give you.

☐ **Use a straw.** A long one, a fat one, a curly one, even a jokey one attached to a hat and dipped into a can of beer. The sillier the better to sip with for fun.

☐ **Pick yourself a go-to karaoke song.** Just know what song you'll ask for should a karaoke stage present itself. Like an emergency candy stash in the cupboard, you may not have to use it, but it's gratifying to have one on hand if you do.

☐ **Read some good news.** Seek out positive stories of assistance, love, redemption, enthusiasm, and plain old luck. Let the good news rise to the top like cream.

☐ **Hum while you walk or whistle while you work.** If it won't bother anyone, the lighthearted whistle will make your job seem lighter and easier. Plus, according to a study by *Choke* author and psychologist Sian Beilock, PhD, of the University of Chicago, it will keep your mind from going into what's called "paralysis by analysis," or thinking so hard that your mental overload makes you choke on a task. Wet your whistle and ease up your mind!

☐ **Press your nose against the window.** A cat can sit and watch life out the window for hours at a time. See how long you can and how much you can find.

☐ **If there's a pig in a blanket at a party, eat it.** Is it good for you? No. Ooh, and what's that, a baby quiche? Try that, too. Delight in trying the big things made little for your palate.

☐ **Use a different-colored bulb.** Switch to a warm yellow one on the front porch, a blue one in the TV room to up the "chill" factor, or use a red bulb to add ambiance to a holiday party.

☐ **Wear your hair in a wildly different way.** Part it on the other side, sweep it over, pull it back, fluff it up, or slick it down. Give yourself a costume change from the neck up.

☐ **If you see a Hula-Hoop, give it a whirl.** It doesn't matter if you can do it or not. It's just that it's nearly impossible to feel sad when you're whipping a plastic tube around your hips like a go-go dancer.

☐ **Sing at the top of your lungs in the car.** Hey, those people you think are judging you will be pulling away when the light turns green anyway. So crank up the volume and let it fly on the highway, as loud as you feel it in your soul. That's what rolled-up windows are for.

☐ **Say, "I'll have what she's having."** Or maybe, "Follow that car!" Choose a line from a classic movie and wait for just the right moment to make use of it. "Maybe not tomorrow, but soon and for the rest of your life."

☐ **Spit the pits.** The best thing I remember about eating watermelon as a kid was how we were allowed to spit the

---

Be Optimistic

See the bright side. Have you ever said, "It's freezing in here" while someone else in the room was actually thinking it was too warm? The world doesn't feel or look the same to all of us—heck, it doesn't even look the same to two people looking at the very *same* thing. As I write about in my book *Bright Side Up: 100 Ways to Be Happier Right Now*, we see what we choose to see. So slip some happy glasses onto your mind and *choose* to see a difficult situation in a positive light. See exciting changes, funny missteps, smiles on strangers, and fresh starts. Here are a few angles to aim for:

- **See the humor.** If you have a disastrous first day of work, you can see a depressing defeat . . . or a really funny story for your future coworkers.
- **See the opportunity.** If your date isn't someone you feel a zing with, you can see it as a failure in love . . . or a chance for a curious conversation with a new pal.
- **See the uniqueness.** On a rainy day, you can see a ruined afternoon . . . or a perfect excuse for the group to pull out a board game.

pits out as we ate. Give yourself the same joy. Eat cherries, grapes, a tangerine, or watermelon outdoors in the grass and see how far you can get the pits to go.

☐ **Make an impression.** In mud. In wet sand. In a pile of twigs you arrange your own way. Stamp a sign in the earth that shows you were here.

☐ **Have a cocktail in the daytime.** Have a mimosa with brunch, a beer with lunch, or an Italian sparkling something before the sun sets. Why? Because it feels like you're breaking the big "rules" of life. Enjoy the moment, with friends beside you and a glass in hand.

☐ **Draw portraits with the person you're with.** You don't have to be a good artist—in fact, it's far funnier if you aren't—to get some joy out of drawing your friend, family member, or partner. Make it a caricature, a stick figure, or an abstract expression of how they seem to you. ("You think my head is that big in *what* way, exactly?") And whether you get laughing or gain some good insights, you win.

☐ **Play with clay.** It feels good to mold and mush clay with your hands, transforming a glob into something useful, beautiful, or, at the very least, unique.

Be Adventurous

Take the leap. I was on an underground cave tour in New Zealand years ago when our guide told us to jump off a rock ledge into water that was completely hidden in darkness. When I finally got the courage to jump, I found out the ledge wasn't very high at all—I had just built up in my mind what I couldn't see with my eyes. And we all do that when faced with challenges: Research shows we fear an unknown outcome more than we do a known *bad* one; it's not the event itself that's scary, but that we don't know *what* it is. Knowing this, battle your fear. The unknown could be the best place you've ever been.

- **Take a running jump.** Take the trip to a new city. Go to the event even if you won't know anyone. Take the job you're only pretty certain you can handle. Jump into the unknown waters, then kick back up to the surface feeling more alive because of it.
- **Attempt what you've always wondered about.** Sing at open-mike night, give a toast, or try your hand at comedy if you've always wanted to. Remember: You don't have to do it twice, and you only live once. Be brave. Because if it makes your knees weak and your stomach churn, it's probably worth it.

☐ **Pick a "favorite" so people know what to get you.** Maybe it's a wine. A flower. A favorite dessert. Or maybe it's a collection of vintage postcards, beach sarongs, or pulp detective novels. Choose what will make people think, "It's just *so* you," when they see it, which makes gifting easy for them, and makes you happy every time.

☐ **Squeeze some water.** Squeeze the plastic trigger on a water gun; get a cool hose attachment for your indoor plants or outdoor garden. Or fill up a water balloon and toss it around. It's satisfying, replenishing, and—like a little taste of summer—totally fun.

☐ **Come up with your own unique tradition.** My friend Jennifer, a mother of three, can never stay awake until midnight on New Year's Eve, so she chooses a country in an earlier time zone and celebrates as they would. One year, they made Moroccan food, played Moroccan music, celebrated at midnight "Moroccan" time, and all got to go to bed early. Invent your own tradition, around the life that works for you.

☐ **Have something bubbly.** A bath. A glass of champagne. A mouthful of candy that pops and sizzles on your tongue.

☐ **Eat a piece of rich, dark chocolate.** Indulge in a few moments of pure, happy bliss. Choose a dark chocolate with a cocoa percent of around 65 percent or higher and keep to about three ounces a day, just enough to get the antioxidant effects of the chocolate's healthy flavanols.

☐ **Have a staring contest with an animal.** It's less intimidating than staring down your friend, and pretty funny considering they have no idea they're even playing. Bet your cat will win!

☐ **Bookmark a website that can turn your day around.** There are thousands of lively ones featuring adorably odd animals who are best friends, or goofy pranks you can't keep from laughing at. Need an idea? Keep the website cuteoverload.com handy to reboot your mood in an instant.

FIVE

Thriving

What fun is the finish line if you haven't completed the marathon? When we feel **productive** and useful, we can be happier. These **bright** ideas will help you **bloom** at work, find **flow** in your passions, and inspire your **dynamic**, creative self.

☐ **Make your first five minutes count.** Purposefully choose the first thing you do in the morning as a symbol for how you want your day to be: Smile. Stretch. Pray. Kiss. Meditate. Breathe. Run. Let the very beginning of your day create the groundwork for the rest.

☐ **Instead of multitasking, do just one thing.** Research shows that when we multitask, we are less efficient at both tasks, because changing your mind-set back and forth tires your mind, making your mental performance weaker all around. So talk to your family at dinner without checking Facebook; drive without talking on the phone; edit your work project without the television on. Give your full focus to one thing at a time.

☐ **Give a day a theme word.** "Courage." "Gratitude." "Laughter." "Joy." Choose a word you want more of, or one that will help you through a particular challenge. Post it on your bathroom mirror, recite it on your way to work, then spend the day bringing that word to life.

☐ **Make two trips from the car or kitchen.** You know that ol' gamble: "Hmmm, maybe I can get all three bowls of soup to the table at once . . ." But your daring attempt is also a stressful one. So the next time you're carrying drippable, breakable, or heavy as heck things, give yourself an extra, lighter trip to make the journey.

☐ **Have a gift card week.** Studies have found that about 5 to 7 percent of gift cards go unredeemed, adding up to around $40 billion or more in unused gift cards. That's like taping a $100 bill to your wall for a dartboard! Collect your cards—from big retailers to online package discounts you couldn't resist. Then pick a week and use them all up.

☐ **Pull a weed the minute you see it.** Life is like weeding a garden. If you pluck a few sprouts a week, starting in June, you won't have brambles on your hands in August. Think of an issue, a mistake, or a resentment with potential to grow big, then grab a little trowel and dig.

☐ **Don't get a new one until you're rid of the old.** You don't need more stuff, especially stuff you don't need. So don't add it your home unless you've subtracted something else.

☐ **Do it your way.** Do something your way, even if it's an unusual way. For instance, I'll never forget the time that a head honcho I was meeting for coffee showed up and said, "I've been sitting all day long; would you mind if we went for a stroll instead?" So we had a window-shopping walk for a meeting. Stand up at your desk, type your proposal draft in purple, or pay your bills while sitting in the park.

☐ **Finish the heck out of something.** Use your shampoo to the last drop, your soap to the last sliver, your hot sauce to the last shake. See yourself wringing out all you possibly can from the item or your energy. Finish that music playlist you promised a friend. Finish sewing that pillow. Finish writing a poem. Finish the race. *Finish it.*

☐ **Watch a spider build a web.** Right before our eyes, spiders will spin their silk into webs to snare their meal or protect their offspring. It seems impossible, and yet they do it, combining beauty and resourcefulness. It can make you think: *What have I built today?*

☐ **Pack a "toy."** We wait for our lunch dates, for our number to be called, for the bus to show up. So give yourself the best chance to make the most of in-between moments by packing yourself a "toy" like a mom would: a magazine, game, or podcast to entertain you even for five minutes at a time. Life is too short to while away your time just waiting.

☐ **Learn a new word in sign language.** Start with the word "hello." With your right hand, form a salute, then move it away from your forehead in a forward motion. Then try the word "friend" by sticking out both of your index fingers— one facing up, one facing down—and take turns tapping your fingers on one another, hooking them together like you're making little finger hugs. And there you have it: "Hello, friend."

☐ **Clean something tonight that will bring you enormous joy tomorrow.** Wash the dinner pots in the kitchen sink tonight, so you can make your morning coffee in a clean space. Or clear off your desk this evening, so you have a blank slate to start on tomorrow.

☐ **Leave fifteen minutes earlier than you think you have to. Just because.** Because sometimes there is traffic or a train delay when you don't expect it. Because sometimes it's hard to find a parking spot. Because then you don't have to rush. Because then you can breathe and be calm and enjoy the journey, instead of stressing about being late.

☐ **Tell an old "up" story.** If you're feeling like nothing good has happened this week, lean on the good that happened last week or last year. Talk to an old friend about that classic dare gone wrong, an embarrassing moment, or your funny trip together one summer. Use your memories for good.

☐ **Put some money into your future.** Put savings into a retirement account—even $5 a month or $100 the next time you have it. My favorite way to save? "Invisibly" invest in a mutual fund or an IRA: Arrange to have a small amount of money (like, say, $50) taken straight out of your checking or bank account every paycheck so you'll barely notice it's going—and ideally, over time, you'll get so used to the transfer, you'll no longer notice at all.

☐ **Upgrade your daily container.** I switched our coin stash from a standard glass bowl to a funny Chiquita banana cookie jar. And you might have a vessel that could use some funning up, too: Give yourself a better rubber band holder, a brighter notebook for your grocery lists, and more beautiful shakers for your salt and pepper.

☐ **"Funnify" something dull in your day.** Pick one groan-worthy thing you do daily and make it more interesting: While you chop vegetables for dinner, pretend you're hosting your own cooking show; while you exercise, watch an episode of a series you love; and while you're walking to work, listen to a chapter of an audiobook. Voilà: You've just replaced a few dull minutes with more engaging ones.

☐ **Think thrice before you post.** We're no longer just what we eat, but what we write. Like carving your initials in wet concrete, our life online is an everlasting symbol of who we are. So slow down and let your thoughts become clear before you share them with the world. You may change your views in the years to come, but the words you write today will live on.

☐ **Answer as many emails as you can in one minute.** Time yourself to respond as quickly as you can. Skip the pleasantries and get to the point; not every email is meant to be answered with a dissertation. "Yup." "Got it." "Will do."

☐ **Make a to-*done* list.** According to the Ziegarnik effect, we tend to remember uncompleted or interrupted tasks more than we do completed ones. Which means you've probably done a lot today—you just don't remember it! If you're feeling like you haven't scratched the surface of your to-do list, put your accomplishments in perspective and make a "to-done list": made lunch, paid the bills, sent RSVP, answered work emails. What you've already accomplished today may be bigger than you think.

☐ **Plant the tiny seed of a larger goal.** You don't have to make a big move toward something you want, just drop a seed: Ask a question, make a call, type it into Google. You'll be surprised what begins to take root.

☐ **Make a "two old" box.** How do you measure what the items in your closet mean to you? Well, by how much you actually use them in life. Fill a box with items you haven't used for two years or more to give to charity or good friends. If you're not loving it, you don't need it.

☐ **Learn how to say your name in the NATO phonetic alphabet.** That's the "Alpha Bravo Charlie . . ." one currently used in aviation and by the military in radio transmissions. It's impressive cocktail conversation and, hey, it might come in handy the next time you find yourself, uh, in an air traffic control tower guiding in a plane to land. I'm Alpha Mike Yankee. You?

☐ **Positively reinforce yourself.** You give a dog a treat when she behaves. Why not treat yourself? Engage in what's called "operant conditioning" by reinforcing your own good behavior. Worked out? You get a frozen yogurt. Finished all your client emails? You get to spend some time scanning the sales on your favorite sites.

☐ **Build your own Work Engagement Ritual.** If I sit down at a clean desk with a hot, strong latte, I trigger my Pavlovian work response: Whether it's five a.m. or ten p.m., it alerts my brain that it's time to be creative and get to work. Find yours. Maybe it's quitting applications on your computer and opening a fresh Word document; maybe it's playing some classical music to calm your mind. Develop a small routine that engages your brain so you'll be raring to go whenever you need it.

☐ **Go cuckoo loco fixo.** You probably have a thing around your house that is driving you so crazy nuts, you can't believe you've let it go for this long. You know: the frame that's always crooked, the sweater with a stray yarn, the headphones held together with tape. Fix it and move on, at last.

☐ **Have a hobby flashback.** When you were a kid, did you used to throw around a softball? Paint with watercolors? Draw cartoons? Kick a soccer ball? Strum a guitar? Revisit your favorite pastimes and see if they still rock your boat.

☐ **Schedule vacation time!** We could all use a reminder to check out. Maybe this will help: Recent surveys have found that Americans leave somewhere between two and nine vacation days behind a year. That's a genie giving you free days for fun! Quick: Take off a Thursday and Friday for a four-day weekend to sleep in, play golf, or see a daytime matinee. Or find a full week three months from now and let your imagination stir after you claim freedom that's yours.

☐ **Make yourself watch ten minutes of a "hard" movie.** Like that foreign film on your Netflix queue or the three-hour classic you've always wanted to see. Do some reconnaissance—just watch just the first ten minutes to see the cinematography, hear the score, get the vibe—and you might just find yourself devouring the whole thing.

☐ **Choose one new vocabulary word and use it three times.** Maybe you open an old dictionary to a random page, or you search for "big words" on Google and pluck one

---

See Progress

Trace the path that got you here. Every experience, class, job, and relationship you've had affects who you are, how you work, and who you love today. So if you're going through a hard time, trust there is a reason that will help you in the future. You may not know why the road is roundabout and rough, but when you reach your destination, the route you traveled will become clear. Here's how to take a new view.

• **Look at what you've learned.** Maybe that job folding sweaters for a neurotic boss gave you the skills to handle high-maintenance clients.
• **Look how much your worldview has widened.** Maybe that art class you took in high school taught you to work more creatively in every area of your life.
• **Look how big your heart has grown.** Maybe that relationship that left you brokenhearted gave you empathy to treat the people you date more kindly today.

from the list. Or let Merriam-Webster's online dictionary choose a Word of the Day for you on their website. To get you started, try the word "galvanize": to startle into sudden activity; stimulate, rouse, stir, spur. Let this galvanize you to use more compelling words when you can.

☐ *Be* **the enthusiasm.** Don't just talk about the enthusiasm you have for something, live it. Animate, elevate, captivate, and engage the people you're talking with about what you really love with the same energy that you *feel* for it. Go big! Show heart!

☐ **For one hour, pretend there's no "later" pile.** The best way to get something off your to-do list is to not let it get on there in the first place. So don't allow yourself a list or pile for "do this later" things. Don't add it to your in-box. Do it now and move on to the next.

☐ **Convert your aggression to progression.** Use your adrenaline for a positive cause: Instead of punching a wall or kicking your printer when you're mad, jab a punching bag or kick it on a disco floor. Instead of running out of patience, go for a run.

☐ **Lower your overhead.** As author Elizabeth Gilbert once wrote, "The smaller you live (materially speaking), the bigger you can live (creatively speaking)." So lower your phone minute limit. Your cable channels. Your electricity usage. Live a big life by spending small. A little slash somewhere can let in the light everywhere else.

Be Flourishing

Choose a "Happiness Measuring Stick." We all have a pair of jeans that help us know when we're gaining or losing weight. So, what's your pair of jeans when it comes to your happiness? What's your measuring stick for how balanced, calm, and happy you really are? For me, it's my garden. When I noticed one busy month that the plants were withering and weeds were taking over, I realized that *I* was buried under, too. After all, what's the point of building a great life if you're too stressed to enjoy it? Your measuring stick will be your happy life's new best friend. So choose yours. What thrives in your life when you're happy? Maybe . . .

- Your houseplants are sprouting; your garden is blooming.
- You see a friend you always make time to have brunch with when life is good.
- Your closet is cleaned out and organized.
- You cook a few times a week, rather than ordering in or microwaving.
- You fit in a regular run or spinning class every weekend.

☐ **Do something preventative.** If you regularly change the oil in your car, you might pay $30 every six months or so. If you don't change it and the engine seizes up? That's thousands of dollars for a new one! Small preventative measures can ward off big fiascos, so make an appointment to check whatever keeps the engine—or bike, or water heater, or your own pumping heart—running.

☐ **Get up without checking the time.** When you wake up, get up, without checking the clock. Have faith the day has woken you when your rest was done.

☐ **Have a housework dance party.** Who says a dance party can only happen on Saturday night? Try the Dirty Dishes Disco and the Latin Laundry Rumba. Use your favorite tunes to give you energy and entertain you while you get the dreary stuff done.

☐ **Flip a coin to choose your path.** Research shows with too many options to choose from, we can get overwhelmed and find it difficult to choose at all. This can lead to either "choice paralysis"—where we freeze and make *no*

Speak Positively

Change your life by changing your words. Life is like ordering from a restaurant menu: You get what you order. So start a habit of using more positive words, little by little. In just thirty days, it might become a natural part of your life.

- **Practice your positive vocabulary.** Flip your language about setbacks. An "awful" day can be "challenging"; a "difficult" client is "teaching you patience"; and getting stuck in "nightmare traffic" is also some "time to reflect."
- **Stop saying you "can't"!** If you're trying to strengthen your willpower, stop using the word "can't." Psychologically saying "I *can't* have dessert" can make you feel like a victim, while saying "I *don't* eat dessert" puts the power back in your hands. It's not that you "can't" do things in life; it's that you choose not to.
- **Build your own "Grumble jar."** Every time you catch yourself saying something negative—or your friends or family alert you to it—put a quarter or $1 in the "Grumble jar," then change what you've said from Grumble to Good.
- **Throw away the negative thoughts about yourself.** *Literally.* A 2012 study out of Ohio State University and a university in Madrid, Spain, found that people who wrote down negative thoughts about their bodies on paper and threw the thoughts away were less influenced by those insecure thoughts later. Toss that silly "garbage" you've been thinking right where it belongs.

decision—or to a lingering regret over the options we left behind. Lighten that pressure on yourself: Narrow your choices down to two, then let a coin toss make the call.

☐ **Read the other side of the argument.** Be your own debate team: Read the reasoning behind the opposing views. It's not about changing your mind; it's about understanding how the other minds feel. Empathy is an asset.

☐ **Make your bed this morning.** It's the simplest way to show your day that you mean business! The night is over, the day has begun, and you're in control, uncluttered in home space and mind. Watch out, world; you're off the mattress and out to make big things happen.

☐ **Outsource something small.** My friend hires someone to fix little things—replace lightbulbs, glue broken chair rails—for an hour or two every other month. Maybe there's something you can get off your hands, too. Barter with a friend: They grab your dry cleaning while you back up their computer.

☐ **Take a "Dream Job" step.** In addition to doing the project that must get done today, do fifteen minutes of something that feeds your dreams of the future. Like "Brainstorm small business ideas" or "Research art program" or "Read one chapter in a business book." Think big, about your to-day and your tomorrow.

☐ **Redefine a reward.** I tricked myself the other day. I said, "As soon as I finish one more hour of work, I'll reward myself with a thirty-minute workout to get my muscles moving." I usually consider a workout grueling, but it changed entirely with that new spin—and when I got go-ing, it felt like a treat for my body, a true reward. Give it a try. Reward yourself with "fortifying" vegetables, the "sat-isfaction" of paying your phone bill, or an errand run that gives you an "escape" from sitting still.

☐ **Clean something you use every day.** Rub your TV re-mote with a Q-tip, wipe down the crevices of your com-puter keyboard, disinfect your home phone, clean your computer cords. A good scrub makes all the difference.

☐ **Get specific if you want to get it done.** If you say "Let's hang out sometime," you might not. But if you say "Let's get spicy tacos next week," your mouth may be on fire by

---

Be Productive

Put an end to procrastination. You know what's worse than putting something off? Kicking yourself all day for how anxious you feel while putting something off! It's doubling the damage. We all suffer sometimes from what the Greeks call *akrasia*, acting against our better judgment by not doing what we *know* we ought to be doing. So here are some ways to suck it up, sit down, bang it out, and get it done.

- **Try "worst goes first."** Get the worst thing off your plate first thing in the morning. Post that phone number on your keyboard so you *have* to call it before you type. Free up your day from carrying that weight on your shoulders.
- **Make it as easy-peasy as possible.** Research has found we have a limited supply of willpower throughout the day, so the less you have to flex that willpower "muscle," the better. If you'll want to work out, lay out your sneakers beside your bed. If you'll want to eat healthier, be sure to have apples in arm's reach.
- **Time it.** You don't want a full day of awful, but you can do ten little minutes, right? Set a timer and make yourself do a task for just that long. You'll either chip away at it ten minutes at a time, or find you're driven to keep on going.

Wednesday. That's because, according to "temporal construal theory," when we make a goal with something specific we can picture in our mind's eye, it seems to belong to the present; while if we frame it abstractly or vaguely, it seems to belong to tomorrow. So the next time you're planning a fun weekend activity, setting a long-term goal, or prioritizing your to-do list, paint a concrete picture and make it happen.

☐ **Shop like a king.** Imagine that you have all the money in the world—plenty to buy what you want today, tomorrow, and the next. Now, this item you're looking at: Do you still want it? Is it flattering or beautiful or perfectly fitting or something you've been searching forever to find? Or does it just seem like a good enough bargain that fills a short-term need? Think grand. Buy only what you love, not what you're persuaded into settling for.

☐ **Reframe your work hours.** If there's a way to shift your work schedule to the hours you'd be most productive, look into it. Can you get one three-day weekend a month, or a Saturday with zero work interruptions? An earlier start, or a later one? Many employers offer flextime options to accommodate not just requirements but preferences for the sake of productivity. Look into it, and shape your work life in a positive way.

☐ **Give a hand to your future self.** What's a cool thing you could give to the "you" six months from now? Some workouts now so the jeans of "future you" fit looser later? A tomato plant now you can pluck from later? Some classes at college now so you'll have a degree later? Be a good pal to the "you" in the future.

☐ **Purge your junk drawer.** Yes, it's *supposed* to be jammed with junk—but not so full that it jams. So empty it out: Toss the pens that don't work and the rubber bands that break when you stretch them, then put back the junk you really may need.

☐ **Identify the smallest, teeniest, shortest step to your goal.** Whether you're building your bank account or climbing Mount Kilimanjaro, taking it small step by small step is the only way to reach great heights. Answer this: What's your destination? Then: Start your journey with one actionable stride that will slowly but surely lead you to the peak.

SIX

Love

We all want to be loved and to **give** love, to have **deep**, true **relationships**. These **tender** ideas will help you build stronger **bonds** in your life—whether it be with a spouse, a family member, a **romantic** partner, or the love you want **more** of in your life.

☐ **Hug two seconds longer.** The real kind; the one where you wrap your arms tight, squinch your eyes closed, and give a good squeeze to stimulate the release of oxytocin, the feel-good, bonding hormone.

☐ **When you think of them, contact them.** People we love pop in and out of our minds all day long, don't they? Buying bread makes us think of one friend; a scary movie preview another—and sometimes, there's no reason at all. Let others know you're thinking of them by texting a short message or giving a quick call. To be thought of is one of the greatest compliments we can get; so pass it along to the people you love.

☐ **Watch the arrivals gate at the airport.** For just a minute, forget about checking in, checking bags, and checking the departure gate for your flight and watch the emotional slices of life happening around you: loved ones embracing each other after days or months or years apart. Traveling is the best when it leads, eventually, to a feeling of home with those you cherish most.

☐ **Ask, "Why *not* me?"** When my friend in New Orleans told me she had her eye on a cute friend of hers, she first thought, "Why would he date me?" Then she bucked up and changed her game. "I realized he was going to date *someone*," she said. "So why *not* me?" My friend and her guy? They're married now. So the same goes for what or who you want: Why *not* you?

☐ **Show compassion.** You don't always need to be someone's first-aid kit fixing it all; when someone shares his or her sadness, just listen. Sometimes it's better to offer your compassion, like a loose bandage that keeps the swelling out, adds comfort, and eases the pain without trying so hard to make it go away.

☐ **When you see someone you love, open your arms wide.** Stretch them out, calling your loved one straight to you, where they can land in the circle of space you've made for them, in the middle of your perfect embrace.

☐ **Send a video message.** Lately, instead of voice mails or emails, my parents have been filming short videos of themselves saying hello, then texting or emailing them to family. It's like the recorded version of Skype, iChat, or FaceTime. And it's fun! Send a personal video that will make it feel like you're in the room for a surprise "hi."

☐ **Forgive some muddy feet.** If someone trails dirt in the house, breaks a glass, or offends your taste, be the bigger person. See how you can make them still feel welcome after their faux pas. Forgive, forget, and move on.

☐ **Build someone else up.** Share how strong someone you love is, how special, how kind, how talented, how wise. Say the things *about* them that they may be too humble to say for themselves.

☐ **If you think of someone to call for their birthday, call immediately.** Not in five minutes. Not when you're done with that work email. Not when it's past dinner in their time zone. Now. As *soon* as you think of it and before you forget, share your good wishes for a great year.

☐ **Feast on a marvelous laugh.** Maybe you have a friend whose laugh is so contagious, it gets you chuckling every time. Or maybe you overhear a stranger snorting, hooting, and huffing, hilariously overtaken with laughter. Appreciate utter glee; it's a gorgeous sound.

☐ **See their hands and feet.** We're used to photographing the faces of people we love—Smile!—but there are other elements so essentially *them*—especially their hands and feet. Spend a minute looking at or photographing this unique aspect of them: your brother's bare feet crossed over the couch arm or kicking back under the table; your grandma's hands holding a book or threading a needle.

☐ **Instead of envy, say, "That will be me."** Look at the people or the couples you want to be like and think, "That will be me. That *will* be me."

☐ **Acknowledge your *jaaneman*.** This Hindi word, pronounced "jahn-eh-mahn," translates as "soul of me." It is a gender-neutral word for your sweetheart, your darling, the one who makes your soul sing. If you have one, hug them. If you're still searching, ask the universe for yours.

☐ **Let someone you love use what is precious to you.** I'm never more touched than when a friend offers to let me drive their new car or wear their favorite necklace. Lend your good headphones. Your designer dress. Your nice camera. Your crystal cake platter. As long as you know your trust in them will make them care for it well.

☐ **Do what *they* want to do.** If you tend to get your way with a particular friend, partner, relative, or kid, offer the gift of giving them *their* way: Watch their TV show; order their favorite pizza toppings; take their route; listen to their song. It might seem like a small gesture, but there's nothing more empowering than being heard.

☐ **Praise a child.** Say, "You're clever. You're marvelous. You're special. You're fun." The words you use to build a kid up can keep them afloat for their whole lives.

☐ **Name one ex who gave you something valuable.** Sure, a lot of exes in love were lousy. But did one pass on a positive gift? Thank them for your appreciation of the opera, a lesson in standing up for yourself, or a child you can't imagine life without.

☐ **Devote a day to someone else.** Sometimes a conflict within yourself can be healed by reaching outward to someone else. If you are struggling, think of how you can use your energies, prayers, or actions to send strength to someone fighting an illness, or confidence to someone taking a big leap. Give away the day with your generous devotion.

☐ **Send someone a handwritten card.** A thank-you note, some sympathy wishes, a congratulations notice, or a birthday card. Even if your handwriting isn't calligraphy, they'll cherish the effort you made with your own hand, more than any typed email could earn.

☐ **Forward an article to someone you love.** Many of us have a parent or relative who sends articles on a regular basis. This week, forward one back or send a link to a friend. Don't just post it, make it personal. It's a "thinking of you" with the added value of a great read.

☐ **Share something that's been eating at you.** It may cause a fight. But if you don't let the piranha out, the issue might eat you from within, silently. Save your insides and your relationship. Let it out.

☐ **Exchange love notes as gifts for a holiday.** When I interviewed singer/songwriter Jewel, she said that for some birthdays or holidays, she and her husband Ty exchange love letters instead of gifts. What a beautiful way to highlight the true meaning of a special day.

☐ **Kiss someone on a spot you cherish, and tell them why.** A dimple you see when they naturally smile; a wrinkle that speaks of the ages you've known each other; hands that cook you dinners of sustenance; an arm that embraces you just right.

☐ **Hug yourself.** It's about as hard to hug yourself as it is to tickle yourself, but go ahead and try. Wrap your arms around one of your own best friends—*you!*—and show yourself how much you care.

☐ **Love the "us."** It's usually right after my friend Todd and I sit back up after being doubled over with laughter that he sighs and says, "I love us." Sometimes the "us" is magic; the ebb and flow, the back and forth, the partnership, the friendship. It's the blending of the two that can make amazing happen. Love an "us" that you have, too.

☐ **Embrace the message, not the mode of communication.** It's so easy to get a message now—no transatlantic flights, no mules carrying mail—that we can forget to appreciate a small message's meaning. But those quick texts, public posts, and cute emoticons still represent an effort to connect. Your network cares. Lucky you.

☐ **Savor the ride.** I recently rode on the back of a tandem bike for the first time, and I struggled with how difficult it was to give up control. Then I realized that instead of fighting for control, I could release it by closing my eyes as I pedaled. So I did; I truly let go and it was magical. Experience this yourself: Close your eyes and trust another person to lead you through the mall, or a few blocks down the street. When someone else is steering—in a car, at a meeting, with your family—let yourself enjoy the ride.

☐ **Buy someone a small treat.** Guess what? Spending small amounts of money on *other* people is good for you. When researchers in a 2008 study out of the University of British Columbia and Harvard Business School gave participants either $5 or $20 and instructed them to spend the money on themselves or others, those who spent the money on others were *happier* than the ones who used it for themselves. So take that five and buy your pal an ice cream.

☐ **Have a "hit by a bus" moment.** How else to appreciate the beginning of a path than to reflect for a minute how sad you'll be when it ends? How better to treat your loved one now than to think how much you'd miss them were they not in your life? None of us know how long we have in life, so do, try, live, and love the most *right now*. By thinking about an ending in the future, you can live up how you love today.

☐ **Leave someone a note.** Leave a note for your friend in their wallet. Leave a note for your child in their lunch sandwich. We often forget what fun it is to get a cute surprise message of kindness.

☐ **Get a relationship role model.** My parents still genuinely love each other's company after forty-plus years of marriage. I'm reminded every time I call and they say, "You know us, we're just partying hard as usual" . . . and then they laugh and go back to watching a Charlie Rose interview with a plate of cookies. Choose a role model in relationships right now: Do they show affection? Build each other up? Balance each other out? Let them inspire you to keep looking for the love you want in your life.

☐ **Let them be their unique selves.** It's not up to us to judge our partner's clothes, our friend's shoes, our parents' hair. They are them, and we are us. Just like the joy children can get from dressing themselves for their first day of school, the beauty comes in letting others show us who they are.

☐ **Make up a secret handshake with someone you love.** The beauty of a true relationship—with a boyfriend, a wife, a BFF—is feeling like the two of you share something together no one else in the world does. Well, then make it official! My husband and I, for instance, have a secret—and hilariously complicated—handshake that we use when we're feeling disconnected or want a good laugh. Create your own private ritual or inside joke that makes your twosome feel awesome.

☐ **Send a random text of kindness.** Think of a friend, co-worker, or school chum who inspires you and send them a kind text, pronto. Like, "Just thinking of you, and it's making me grin." Or, "Feeling inspired by your go-get-'em attitude right now." Or "You're amazing and I miss you." Imagine how good you'd feel if *you* got that message? Your missive might stick with them for good.

☐ **Tell someone, "You can do it."** Sometimes it's someone *else's* faith in you that propels you toward the finish line— or the start. Say, "I believe in you. You can do it."

☐ **Find an older couple holding hands.** Witness the caring of people who have lived through more of life than you, for whom love today helps carry them through.

☐ **Make your next choice from a loving place.** The choices we're most likely to regret are the ones we make for the wrong reasons—the job we take purely for the money, or the date who seems "great on paper" but doesn't make our heart sing. So make your next choice from a place of pure kindness. If you're wondering if you should date someone, ask yourself, "Is there true caring here?" If you're wondering which career to pursue, ask, "Will I love waking up to do this every day?"

☐ **Fetch their slippers.** I love the old-fashioned idea of bringing someone a pair of slippers and a cup of tea—as long as you both give equally to each other. Dote on your partner, your parent, your friend. What a luxury for them to be

---

Be Curious

Get to the heart of someone you love. When my dental hygienist Maya cleaned my teeth some months ago, she told me how her husband Jack had passed away of liver disease. Though they'd been together for ten years, it was in his final weeks that she said to him, "What do you want to talk about? What do you want to say to me?" They spent his last three weeks having nightly talks about their families, their spirituality, and their fears. "I have no regrets," Maya told me, as my tears dripped onto my dental bib. Except, she added, "I wish we'd talked about all these things sooner." Learn more about someone *you* love, too, from the inside out.

- Ask, "What was your proudest moment as a child?" Tap into their innocence.
- Ask, "What's your biggest fear?" This opens the door to their soul.
- Ask, "What do you believe in?" Understand what their life means by what they believe their life becomes.
- Ask, "What do you think is your life's purpose?" Don't assume their core beliefs; *ask*.
- Ask, "What do you wish you were good at?" Open the window to their dreams.

---

served with such kindness from you, without expecting anything in return.

☐ **Don't be a help-o-phobe.** The *very* next time someone offers to help you in some way, accept it. When you're cleaning up after the party. When you're carrying luggage to the car. When you can't translate the wine menu. Let someone lift and clean and carry and recommend. You don't have to do it all. In fact, if you do one thing less, it'll feel really darn good.

☐ **Hold a kitten.** Or just pet one. Or, heck, just watch one in a video on YouTube. One minute of all that tiny, fluffy goodness and your heart can't help but swell with love.

☐ **Act in honor of their memory.** Think of someone you loved and miss dearly on this earth today. What would make them happy to see you do? What would make them proud? What would be something *they* would do if they could? Do it in their honor: Run. Raise. Climb. Love. Feed. Help. Laugh. Don't just miss them, live *through* them.

☐ **Write "11 Things I Love About You."** That's an easy way to get you started on a modern love letter to your partner, your parent, or your very best friend. Share lots of little things about them that have changed your life forever.

☐ **Offer an internal compliment.** Give someone a compliment that really speaks to the core of who they are. Never mind their shoes or hair; tell them how much you admire their fortitude, are inspired by their creativity, or wish you had a fraction of the courage they show every day.

☐ **Support your tribe.** Today, think about the team you're a part of, and support one another to succeed together, rather than excelling on your own. Couples: Be your own best friends, standing strong hand in hand. Families: Be a tribe.

☐ **Share *un recuerdo*.** In Spanish, this means "a memory." And I loved this little idea actress Salma Hayek once shared about it. She said when she goes out, her young daughter "gives me something to remember her," Salma said. "She calls it *un recuerdo* and it changes all the time. She sneaks it into my bag so it's a surprise!" Share your own "memory"

Go Deep

Get "coning." One of the tenets of "emotionally focused therapy"—known as EFT—is that all of our actions are really a response to the emotions underlying them. We may give a cold shoulder, but it's really because we're scared, jealous, or sad. My mother, Katherine, an EFT-certified therapist, likened it this way one day: "Picture it like an ice cream cone," she said. "Most interactions are like the ice cream on top. The goal is to dig deeper until you get to the hidden part at the tip of the cone." The deeper you go into the *why* of someone's behavior, the more you'll understand *who* they really are. To make sharing sweeter:

- **Make physical contact so the other person feels safe.** Opening up is hard because we feel vulnerable. Help your loved one feel protected by connecting physically: Hold their hand, rub their back, touch their knee.
- **Redefine the anger.** Anger is one of the easiest emotions to turn to, but it's often a disguise for the hurt that lies underneath: When we're angry that a boyfriend came home late without calling, it's really because we're *hurt* he didn't think about us waiting at home, right? Next time, imagine that an angry reaction is them or you really saying, "I'm hurt." Then reconnect from there.
- **Respond from a place of love.** You might not like what you're hearing, but instead of shouting, "See? You *always* do this!" consider what you're feeling, which might sound more like: "This makes me scared that we're drifting apart, and I love you and I don't want that."

with someone you love. Maybe it's a note you've kissed, a piece of candy, or a playing card from your favorite game.

☐ **Do one "Be a Good Friend" deed.** If you ever think how lucky you are to have good friends, *be* a good friend. Do one thing today that a good friend would do. Drop off soup to

---

Be Snuggly

Touch the person you love. Do you know the story of the "rescuing hug"? It began when twins Kyrie and Brielle Jackson were born prematurely at a Massachusetts hospital in 1995, weighing just two pounds each. One day, Brielle was having a turbulent day alone in her incubator, so a nurse laid the twins side by side; and when Kyrie put her tiny arm around her sister, Brielle's blood oxygen levels rose, her breathing steadied, and she survived. Human touch isn't just for our romantic partners. **Offer your own rescuing touch** when someone seems lost or lonely. **Rub someone's feet**, their hands, their shoulders, their scalp. And if you want to keep your relationship monogamously healthy? **Embrace them.** In a 2012 study out of Germany, men who were given a dose of the bonding hormone oxytocin were more likely to avoid standing next to a woman they'd just met—and the best way to get the oxytocin flowing is with one long, true hug.

---

someone who isn't feeling well; text a goofy video link to a colleague who could use some cheering up; or take out a pal who needs some company.

☐ **Keep a secret.** It's so tempting to share that secret with *just* one more person. Don't. Truly and honestly keep it to yourself. We share our deepest feelings with friends because we feel safe. Protect your friend by keeping their secret to yourself.

☐ **Give someone a chance to show you how they excel.** We all want to be noticed for what we're best at but don't always get the chance to show it. Give someone you care about the opportunity to ace it where they can.

☐ **Flatter that friend who drives you nuts.** Instead of gearing up to find the flaw in everything your friend says, start the interaction with something positive. Maybe it's "You're one of the quirkiest people I know" or "You have such a go-get-'em personality, it inspires me." Offer them honey and you just might draw their sweet side out.

☐ **Say "I'm sorry."** None of this "I'm sorry you feel that way" or "I'm sorry it didn't work out." Just "I'm sorry," plain and simple. Apologize from the heart, and move on.

☐ **Devote yourself.** The Japanese have a word for expertise that develops from the repetition of a process over many years: *shokunin*, the art of mastering something, so you can provide the best for the people receiving your work. Is there anything you're drawn to? A skill you can hone? Show some devotion to a craft that can benefit others. You may not become a master, but it feels good to learn.

SEVEN

Effervescence

A vital element to a happy life is a strong **bond** to your **community**. These **socially** driven ideas will help you strengthen your **connections**, as well as true relationships with **friends**, family, neighbors, and new **people** you meet.

☐ **Acknowledge your twinsies.** If you're in a red Kia car and they're in a red Kia car, you guys should be friends for the 2.4 seconds you pass by each other on Main Street. If you've chosen the same sneakers, the same sweater, or the same cell phone case as someone you meet, applaud yourselves. "Hi, there," you can say with a nod. "We have such good taste."

☐ **Wave at firefighters.** Somewhere between Tonka toy characters and today, firefighters have become part of the quilt of our life. We may not notice them—let alone thank them—but we should. Give the next one you see a friendly wave to express how much you appreciate their courage and service.

☐ **If a street musician makes you happy, stop and listen.** If the tune makes your soul jump, stop, and bask in it, even for five minutes. You're letting a performer be heard, and you're giving your spirit a front-row seat to happiness.

☐ **Make a baby giggle.** It's such a simple joy to see that innocence and hear that joy, the clearest evidence of instant pleasure. And whatever makes the baby giggle? Keep doing it.

☐ **Radiate the room with your smile.** Thanks to the power of "empathic resonance," when others see *you* smile, it can send signals to their brains that *they* are happy and they may end up smiling back. See how long you really have to hold yours before you warm up another person in the room. You may even start a chain reaction, from one person to the next, all the way to the onion dip.

☐ **Go to a Pee Wee game.** Unlike televised sports—built around advertising dollars and sponsored athletes—watching kids play a game can transport you to a more innocent time. Vicariously experience their nervous flutters before they step up to bat, watch their legs kick, and listen to their screeches of joy. Did *you* once feel this? Can you find it for yourself again?

☐ **Do a block full of walk-ins.** You know those weird little shops you always pass by and never go in? Make it your mission to enter. Walk one block on foot and step into each and every place you hit from the hair salon ("Just wanted to say hi!") to the vacuum cleaner repair center ("In case I need a fix"). Make it your mission to know what's really in your neighborhood.

☐ **Buy a coffee twin.** You've seen this in the movies: A character walks into another's office with two cups of java, saying, "Hey, brought ya a cup of coffee." But how often are we doing it ourselves? Tomorrow, get two coffees: one for you and one for a friend—and when you see them, well, you know what to say.

☐ **Be a "flower" child.** You can warm up your one space with a dozen seasonal flowers, or you can warm up a *dozen* people's spaces with *one* flower each from the same bunch. Grab a bouquet and hand out the buds, to friends in the office or strangers on the street. What a sweet random joy that would be, a colorful bloom out of the blue.

☐ **Make a new happy friend.** Research has shown that moods are "contagious," so if you surround yourself with positive people, their energy will rub off on you. So make it your mission to forge one optimistic new friendship with someone who will encourage you to see the bright side and keep living toward your dreams.

☐ **Eat a full meal out without checking your phone or email.** Need some extra incentive? Play smartphone roulette. After you and your mates sit down, pile your phones in the middle of the table; if anyone touches or checks their phone before the bill comes, they pay the damage. It's a good reminder: Our experience eating out should be about appreciating our companions, our environment, and the food in front of us. What's there in the moment wins.

☐ **Do right by your *ichariba chodei*.** This Japanese saying means, "When we meet, we become family." It is a sense that your friends feel like family in spirit, and that you'll do them no harm. Who are your "family friends"? Would it be nice for them to hear that you see them that way?

☐ **Talk to someone who really needs to talk.** I was on an airplane recently, when the woman next to me shared at takeoff that she'd gone through a breakup and was feeling pessimistic about her future. "Well," I said with a laugh, "you sure sat next to the right person!" I let her share and I offered what I could. But sometimes just being an ear for others when they need it is enough.

☐ **Go to a festival.** I promise: There is a celebration of something you love *somewhere*. Hit a garlic festival. A garden festival. An outdoor music one. Or pick an event devoted to lobsters, art, beer, strawberries, telescopes, or hot-air balloons and plan around it. Gather with like minds to feast on what you love.

☐ **Bring someone you want to impress to a bright place.** Studies have found that we may unconsciously impose the elements of a place—romantic, serious, dark, fun—onto the person we are with. Use this to your advantage and let a space help speak for you.

☐ **Sing along to someone else's birthday.** When the table behind you erupts into the "Happy Birthday" song, and those servers join in procession with candles on a cake, enhance their occasion. Sing along. Make someone's celebration one voice louder.

☐ **Have "the most important conversation."** By this, I mean that instead of chatting up your usual suspects, talk to the person who seems to need it *most*. Maybe it's the person standing alone at the baby shower. Or the one who isn't saying much in the group discussion. Or the person who seems especially sad at the picnic. Don't have just any conversation; have the most *vital* one. Because that's when you have the greatest opportunity to make a difference with your presence.

☐ **Use words from the "happy" list for your next online post.** When researchers at the University of Vermont scanned through ten million American Twitter posts to find the happiest places in the country (Hawaii and Maine topped the states), they did so by noting people's tweets of positive words—especially words like "rainbow," "LOL," "good," "nice," "sleep," "wine," and beach-related or food-related words. Well, I don't know about you, but put me on a good beach under a rainbow with a nice glass of wine and I'm happy, LOL. There. Now try a positive post yourself!

☐ **Get to know the name of locals in your hood.** That barista at the coffee shop and that server in the diner? Those are your people and it will feel rewarding to greet them that way. "You know," you might say, "I see you every morning and I've never asked your name." Then move through your mornings mindfully, greeting those who care for you personally.

☐ **Join a club.** According to research by Robert D. Putnam, professor of public policy at Harvard University, joining a club that meets just once a month can extend your life and have the same impact on your happiness as doubling your income. Try a book club, a bike club, a quilt club, or a "Let's all watch the latest episode of this show together" club. Enrich your life through a regular connection with a community of your peers.

☐ **Count ten smiles in the room.** Be the surveillance camera of happiness and play the "I spy" game of big grins. Try to find ten smiles in the room or on the street. Biggest face beam wins.

☐ **Vow to talk to every person who talks to you first.** At a work conference, on the train platform, at the bar. For one day, if they say hi, decide you're in for at least a minute. You never know where it could lead.

☐ **Delete a dud.** Is there a name you scroll past on your phone who you'd rather not have to see? Delete it. You only need to "call" on people who bring out your best.

☐ **If they like it, give it to them.** In some cultures, from Africa to the Middle East, it is said that if you compliment someone on an item, they may feel compelled to give it to you. It's amazing to imagine. *What would that be like?* To give

---

Be Open

Open up your body language. I was at the grocery store when a well-meaning older man said, "Hey, smile!" I was confused until I gave myself a look-see. And, gosh, there I was: hunched over, with my arms crossed, and my brow furrowed; I *did* kind of look like I was planning to accost the kiwis. It reminded me how much our body language and our feelings are intertwined. Just as our happy thoughts affect our body language, we can employ "embodied cognition" so that our body language can affect our thoughts: If you want to feel happy, *stand* happy; if you want to feel open, *act* open. Shift your body to take the good stuff in.

- **Look up:** Lift up your chin when you walk and set your sights on the world ahead of you and above you, where hopeful things happen.
- **Uncross yourself:** Uncross your arms or your legs so that instead of shielding your body, you're exposing it. Take your hands out of your pockets when you're waiting for someone; face the room, not the corner.
- **Make eye contact when you speak.** Even two or three seconds of direct eye contact and a warm smile will lead to more positive interactions with those around you.

away something you cherish to a person who admires it? Try this once. You've worn it, written with it, read it. So now try, "You like my pen? Keep it."

☐ **Accept a free taster from the tester.** If they're offering free tastes, take one; it's not a contract. Their job is not to sell more items; it's to spread the word—and they're doing it by giving free food to you. Help them succeed by having a bite!

☐ **Ask only open-ended questions for ten minutes.** At work or out socially, challenge yourself to avoid yes or no questions that shut down a conversation quickly. Try "How's today going?" or "What's your story?" or "Tell me about your last twenty-four hours." Engage others first in a positive way.

☐ **Get a party trick.** My friend David can balance an egg on end. My friend Beth can still hit the floor and do "the worm"—with the bruises to show for it two days later. If you don't have a party trick, find one you can do for an "Oooh!"

☐ **That person who's always the happiest to see you? Spend fifteen minutes with just them.** Your dog, wagging its tail? Your nephew who wants to play trucks? A fan of your work who gets giddy talking to you? Give them some of your time. You know they'll use it with care.

☐ **Have courage, my friend.** Go ahead, let someone laugh at you, misjudge you, or decide you're not enough for them. Then walk away with your head held high, knowing with profound certainty that the ones left standing by and supporting you are the ones who are meant to be yours.

☐ **Make a friend who's not your own age.** It's healthy to have friends of all ages: older, wiser friends who can teach you what they've learned; and younger ones who can remind you to let go and loosen up for the ride of your life.

☐ **Acknowledge the person who sometimes becomes invisible in their job.** Like the person who buses your dirty dishes, the attendant who takes your fee, the sanitation worker picking up your trash. We are all interlocking pieces of life's big puzzle, and we need each other. *See* them. Thank them.

Be Bountiful

Put a comparison in perspective. Is there someone you envy for seeming to have it all? Well, what makes others happy isn't necessarily what works for you. So the next time you find yourself feeling envious, reflect on the true riches you have yourself.

- **Coveting their goods?** Remember: Big homes cost more to heat and expensive cars cost more to fix. Maybe what you have right now is just right for you.
- **Coveting their looks?** Life isn't "one size fits all." You're a different height or shape or age, so what looks good on someone else is not supposed to look good on you! Pick what's enviable about your appearance and show it off.
- **Coveting their relationship?** All you're seeing is their high-light reel of love. Every relationship has ups and downs, whether you see them or not, and you're meant to have your own uniquely riveting ride.

☐ **Make one person belly laugh.** Professional comedians know the joy that comes from cracking up a room. Feel that for yourself! Share a funny story. Do a goofy dance. Put on a pink wig for dinner. Take an embarrassing dare. It's rejuvenating to be responsible for someone else's laughter.

☐ **At your next party, branch out thrice!** When actress Judy Greer was on one red carpet, she shared her plans for a party she was hitting with her husband. "We always try to talk to three people we don't know," she said, "so I'm excited to see who the three people will be." Now *that's* a happy attitude. Try it! Force yourself to branch out.

☐ **Support a mom-and-pop shop.** Today, choose the local, family-owned business that's weathered the years over the big-box version up the street. Patronize the small coffee spot, the tiny bike shop, or the old-fashioned pizza place and show them you're glad they're still here.

Be Insightful

Supersize the small talk when you meet a new person. Instead of swapping tales about the weather with a stranger, go deeper. Find out what makes them tick, what makes them laugh, and maybe what even moves their soul. You can get to know someone better in a short time with the right questions. Try asking some of these:

- "What's the best thing that happened to you today?"
- "What are you absolutely awful at?"
- "What's the last brave thing you did?"
- "What makes you happy?"
- "What would you love to do on your next day off?"

☐ **Clap for someone.** If a server's save of a toppled glass impresses you, clap. If a toddler wobbles their way across the sidewalk, clap. If a street juggler catches all the balls, clap. We all feel good when we're recognized, so applaud your peers for small, pleasing jobs well done.

☐ **Ask your friends what's most annoying about you.** And sheesh, if they're brave enough to answer? Stop doing the annoying thing. Try it.

☐ **Step off the judges platform.** We've all misjudged someone, right? So the next time you feel someone is misjudging *you*, forgive them for it. What comes around may have gone around before. So back up, forgive it, and let it go.

☐ **Distract yourself from worrying about how you look or sound.** For every minute you're feeling self-conscious about yourself in public ("Am I standing the right way?" "Do I sound smart enough?"), you're missing a chance to connect with people. The second you catch yourself feeling self-conscious, focus on the essence of someone *else*.

☐ **Make food to bring to others.** Feeding those we care about is an act of love. So make a batch of cookies, cupcakes, candies, flavored popcorn, or a nut mix and give it all away—for no other reason than wanting to nourish the people you like.

☐ **Look people in the eye for three seconds when you say thank you.** Elevate the phrase like you would if you'd just learned it in a foreign land and are using it consciously. *Mahalo* in Hawaiian. *Merci* in French. *Tak* in Danish. *Thank you.* Make it meaningful.

☐ **Bet a friend.** Betting on something invests you in it— whether money is changing hands or not. So go all in . . . or maybe just a chip or two! Bet a free lunch for your weight-loss goals. Bet a pedicure for the first person to get their taxes done. Don't break the bank, just make a simple activity a little more fun.

☐ **If you love your server, add a dollar.** When you're tipping a server who has uplifted your day, work out the right tip, and then—at the end—add a dollar. It's only a tiny in-

Be Supportive

Make them feel heard. While talking to a woman at a recent barbecue, I noticed that she spent our entire five-minute conversation looking over my shoulder, then excused herself to go laugh with some people in the kitchen. I don't think she meant anything personal by it, but I couldn't help but feel like I'd disappointed her in some way, that I wasn't exciting or interesting enough to justify her time. *Gosh*, I remember thinking, *I hope I don't make other people feel that way.* Because it's not always the words we exchange with people that matters; it's also how we feel in one another's presence. Try to make people feel like they're the only person in the room, like they matter. Because you know what? They do.

crease in what you were already giving, but it symbolizes a grander thank-you. Your good dollars will come back to you in karma spades.

☐ **Don't interrupt.** Sometimes we so badly want to communicate that we *totally* understand the person we're talking to that we . . . well, we butt in. Today, pick one conversation where you won't interrupt. Take it in before you take your turn.

☐ **Ask someone older than you what he or she loves most about the area you're in.** Whether you're visiting a new town or asking about the one you're in, you'll get some great history and appreciation for where you are and what's best.

☐ **Be the waver-on.** Be the driver at the stop sign who lets the other car go first. Be the subway passenger who allows another person to step onto the car before you. Be the cyclist who encourages a pedestrian to cross the street first. Be first and insist. You may lose a few seconds in the moment, but you'll gain a good feeling that lasts for hours.

☐ **Thank your friends publicly.** My high school friend Arianna regularly posts what she calls "Grateful Friends Daily" online. She tags a friend, lists all the things she's grateful for—like, "You are fun and outgoing" and "You have a positive outlook"—and then she ends it with, "For this, I admire you." Try it yourself and see how good it feels.

EIGHT

Tranquility

What good is the good life if you aren't **relaxed** enough to appreciate any of it? These **peaceful** ideas will help you keep **balance** in your life, calling in moments of **calm** so you can **unwind** in the **paradise** of your own body and mind.

☐ **Put your feet in the water.** Let it transport you. Close your eyes while the water collects around your feet or the tide washes over your ankles. Kick it, splash in it, and revere in the beauty of a body of water bigger than your bathtub, where you can wade in with your bare toes for one minute or ten. This isn't something you can do at your desk, or in your car, or running errands. This is a moment. *Step into it.*

☐ **Leave your phone behind for half a day.** This is truly challenging, but worth it. For as you look to pass the time on the sandwich line, the bus stop, or waiting for a meeting to start, you'll have nothing to focus on but the people around you and the thoughts in your mind. Take in what you see, hear, and feel.

☐ **Light that candle.** If you were to ask that candle decorating your bookcase what it really wanted, it would probably say, "Please, light me!" Allow the candle to do what it was created to do. Lend it a match and let it shine.

☐ **Close your eyes and swim into the light.** There aren't many times you get to do this one, but I promise it's worth it: The next time you're swimming in a pool, a creek, or the open sea with the sun shining low, close your eyes and swim into it. It feels what heaven might be like, just floating there, into the sun's warm hands.

☐ **Take a leisurely left.** We're always rushing to make that turn at the intersection, timing it so we can just slip through. Next turn, take your time. Sit back. Wait for a big space. Ease on through.

☐ **Name your favorite imperfection.** The Japanese concept of *wabi sabi* encourages acceptance of the imperfections of things. There will always be asymmetry, lumps, and bumps in life, and if we can see the beauty in our ever-flawed world, we give a gift to ourselves. Seek the *wabi sabi* in yourself when you look in the mirror, or at the person you love, or on the mug you use. That chip or drip or freckle is what stands out from all the rest. That is true beauty, indeed.

☐ **Forgive someone their bad mood moment.** The next time someone snaps or cuts you off or cuts in front of you, imagine yourself handing them a "Get-out-of-jail-mood-free card" by not taking it personally. It probably isn't you. And as Mom might say, "You're not mad at them, you're mad at how they behaved." And she *was* always right, wasn't she? Let it go.

☐ **Listen to the music of the rain.** Rain may fall silently, but it lands with lovely sounds: in the street, the gutters, your flowerpots. Listen to the beat, the subtle notes it plays; a symphony of rain, just passing through.

☐ **Unsubscribe to an email list.** There. Doesn't that feel good? You were never taking advantage of those sales or offers anyway. Your in-box just got lighter, which means your to-do list of deleting just got smaller.

☐ **And . . . unsubscribe to another one.** Even lighter, less, and very free.

☐ **Plan an unplanned day.** Sometimes we spend an entire day off completely *on*: getting errands done, laundry cleaned, and groceries bought. Give yourself a true day off and plan to make no plan. Sleep in late. Take a walk. Read a magazine. Allow yourself time to get places. Do something different or nothing at all.

☐ **Skip a stone.** If you're at the water with stones and your feet, the universe is asking you to toss a rock and try for a double skip.

☐ **Clean off one surface in your home—for good.** Clear your coffee table of clutter, or empty your desk of everything but your laptop, or keep a spot on the kitchen counter always open for a cutting board to chop an onion. If you clear your space, you'll clear your mind.

☐ **Seek ambient sounds in real life.** You know those sounds they put on sleep machines to set on your bedside table? Go have a listen in real life: Find a babbling brook. Chirping birds. Crashing waves. They'll be even richer in person.

☐ **Put lotion on a dry spot.** Picture a dry, desertlike spot on your skin, cracking in the heat and thirsting for moisture.

Add a dollop of lotion, rub it in, and imagine your skin saying, "Ahhhh."

☐ **Play the music of absolutely nothing.** This time when you walk, do it to the music of the street. This time when you hike, do it to the music of the trees. This time when you write or paint or rest, do it quietly. Let life itself sing to you.

☐ **Turn down your covers before you go to bed.** Prepare yourself a space, pillows readied, comforter turned down and open to envelop and hug you, so you can slip right in.

☐ **Find something in the clouds.** As children, we found fairy tales in the clouds. What do you see right now? Maybe angels in the wispy ones. Maybe a zebra in the cotton-like cumulus. Or maybe you just see one big layer of gray that doesn't budge, anticipating the hour when the blue peeks through.

☐ **Streeeetch.** Maybe you do ten minutes of flowing Vinyasa yoga moves to limber up, or maybe you just bend over and slowly round your back. Stretch your calves, your thighs, and your arms over your head and across your body.

☐ **Stop and smell the roses.** Or the honeysuckle. Or the flowers on the gardenia or lilac bush. There's a reason this idea gets passed along; it's worth it! Hold still your feet and engage your nose. It only takes a second. You have time.

☐ **Float.** In a bathtub, in the sea, on a raft anchored in a lake. Feel the undulation of the water beneath you, the magic of the earth's invisible glass holding you up.

☐ **Feel the sun on your face.** A few minutes of pure, SPF-free light on our skin is good for us, as the UVB rays in the sun stimulate our skin to produce vitamin D, which is good for our bones and a healthy nervous system and can up our mood. Step out of the shade on a chilly day, close your eyes, and feel the sun on your eyelids, warming your cheeks, seeping into your soul.

☐ **Have a swim, then fall asleep.** It's the peanut butter and chocolate of actions; they go perfectly together. The next time you have an opportunity, plunge into the sea, then collapse under the sun on the sand. Or splash and do laps in a pool, then rinse off for a sweet, short nap. Float in the water, then lay flat on the earth.

☐ **Frame your own "Vacation Monet."** Where are your vacation photos? Stored in a scrapbook or saved in a computer file? Turn one that gives you peace into a piece of art by enlarging and framing it. Display your favorite shot of the mountains, a lake, a cobblestone street, or a fountain in the sun. Relive one of the best sights of your life every day.

☐ **Breathe in lavender.** The flowering plant is like a natural stress reducer, as multiple studies have found the aroma of *Lavandula hybrida* to lessen anxiety in dental patients and students. Try some essential oil, scented soap, or sprigs of the purple flower to calm you down.

☐ **Give yourself a chill chair.** We should all have a spot in our home or near it, where the only thing that happens is relaxation. Maybe it's your bed, a swing, or a nook in the window. Make yours a no-work, no-stress zone. Nothing but "chillaxing" allowed.

☐ **Ooze into something a little too much.** Stretch languidly on the couch for longer than usual. Watch too many episodes of a show you like in a row. Eat three too many cookies. You're a grown-up, remember? You *get* to.

☐ **Do the "muscle mash."** Squeeze your own shoulders, massage your own forearms after all that typing, or lay down a tennis ball and rest your aching spine along it. Your muscles will leave you a big ol' imaginary tip.

☐ **Cook some comfort food.** Bake some biscuits or some brownies, or make mashed potatoes or mac and cheese. Serve up a dish that makes all the stress of the day melt away at the sight of it.

☐ **Simplify something in your life.** Create a "task funnel" by making a few payments automatic or combining two credit accounts into one. Post your grocery list on your fridge with a handy pen. Buy a pill case for your daily vitamins so you won't forget to take them. Make something easier to take the pressure off your mind.

☐ **Take a "vacuum cleansing" breath.** Close your eyes and imagine your nose as a little vacuum cleaner pulling in a cleansing breath. Inhale, slowly and deeply, and let the fresh, new air swirl around inside your head as clean as a hardwood floor. Then exhale it all out. Your mind, dust bunny–free.

☐ **Massage your face when you moisturize.** Our jaws are working hard all day long, with all that chomping and talking—and if you're stressed, maybe some clamping and grinding thrown in, too. Massage as you moisturize.

☐ **Give yourself the star spa treatment.** You needn't spend big to feel special. Give yourself an at-home facial mask. Or a manicure or pedicure. Or a hot-oil hair treatment. Save money and treat yourself well.

☐ **Record the background sound of your happy life.** Last summer, I recorded thirty minutes of the sounds from the back deck of my summer shack: birds chirping, small planes flying overhead, the wind rustling the grapevines. Now, if I awake from a toss-and-turny sleep, I will play it in my headphones to soothe myself with the sounds of my

Be Free

Play hooky. It was about ten years ago that I took my "social sabbatical." I was single and working hard to build my career, but I was becoming overwhelmed by the dinners, drinks, and work functions on my schedule, because I wasn't able to fit in one of the things that meant the most to me: writing. So that month, I told my friends I was taking what I was calling a "social sabbatical." Like professors or professionals who take a temporary hiatus to head into the world, I planned one to step *out* of it. For one month, I came straight home after work and spent each night quietly working on a book (which eventually became my first book, *Meeting Your Half-Orange*, about how to use dating optimism to find your other half in love). When I joined the world again a month later, being social felt even sweeter after the time away. Sometimes we need to step *out* of the routine we're in, in order to be our best selves when we climb back in. Free yourself the same way. **Take your own "social sabbatical"** for a weekend or more to tune back in with yourself. **Play hooky** from work, a party, or a stressful family function. Or **escape on a micro-retreat** by house-sitting a friend's place or checking into an inexpensive hotel room where you'll feel like you've snuck off to freedom.

favorite place. Capture thirty full minutes of what *you* love: friends laughing, kids playing, your father talking. In the future, the sounds of today may relax you.

☐ **Take a bath in the dark.** Create a cave of bliss, like your own Yucatán *cenote*, where you can soak in unlit luxury. Add oils, bubbles, or the soft light of one candle and play soft music or none at all. Burrow into the warmth to ease away your troubles underwater.

☐ **Find the "extra" in the ordinary.** Those tiny flowers sprouting from cracks on the ground are as beautiful as the ones in the garden. Those proud hydrants steeling themselves on sidewalks are symbols of a bustling city. The average can be more if we choose to see it that way.

☐ **Do "nothing" for two minutes.** It's a longer time than you think, but try it: Set a timer and let yourself be, or go to the site donothingfor2minutes.com to try it online. It will be hard not to pick up your phone, or tap your fingers, or write down what comes to mind ("Shoot, I have to call the bank!"). But try it. This mini-meditation can calm you to your toes.

Chill Out

Diffuse your anxious thoughts. If you bump your head, you put ice on it so it doesn't swell up, right? Well, studies have shown we can do the same thing with our thoughts. When we get caught up in negative thoughts, our brains actually "heat up" in a way, too, sending more blood flow to certain parts of the brain, which makes it harder for us to make rational decisions. Clinical psychologist Bruce Hubbard, PhD, even calls an emotionally charged idea that breeds negativity a "hot thought." But with practice with "cognitive restructuring"—essentially shifting your own thoughts to change your mind—you can learn to "cool" your head. Ways to try:

- **"Name it to tame it."** According to research by Matthew D. Leiberman and David Creswell of UCLA, naming an emotion—like "fear," "stress," or "jealousy"—can calm down those excessively aroused circuits in your emotional brain. Call it what it is so you can deal and move on.
- **Talk to yourself like you'd talk to a friend.** We are kind and encouraging to people we like—so tell yourself what you'd tell a close friend.
- **Put a negative thought on trial.** Question your "hot thought" like a good lawyer. Are you *really* going to lose your job if you're a few minutes late for one meeting? No. Diffuse the flame headed to the dynamite.
- **Do "the interrupter."** When a negative thought enters your mind, close your eyes and envision someone's palm reaching out to say stop, or picture a big red stop sign. Stop the thought. Reverse it. Then try again.

☐ **Listen to your silence.** How can you make it even quieter?

☐ **Give a nod to the *rightness* of everything.** You may wish you had more love, more money, more responsibility, more hardwood floors; you may dream of a vacation away, a romantic partner, a better car, or a bigger house. But right now, think how maybe, just maybe, where you are is just where you are supposed to be.

☐ **Take a walk through the forest.** Japanese researchers have found that a walk through the trees can lower your stress hormones more than a stroll through city streets. They call this "forest bath" *Shinrin-yoku*, a taking in of the atmosphere and earthy fragrance of the woods. So find a quiet path in the woods, where trees tower above you, and take a "bath" in the evergreens.

☐ **Do something positive before bed.** Sleep with happy thoughts, not I-just-watched-a-scary-zombie-TV-show ones. Dream easy.

☐ **Let go of the outcome.** You can put your coin in the gumball machine, but life chooses what color you get. Be like the Buddha holding your quarter: Be at peace with your outcome, whatever it may be.

☐ **Embrace footie freedom.** You know that feeling when you take off your shoes after a long day or an endless stand-up night? Freedom is best felt after some constriction, when you kick off your heels and can hear your toes singing. Exhale and wiggle away.

☐ **Wind down with a presleep routine.** If you read or take a warm bath before you go to bed, your body will come to see these as signals of sleep and will start to relax. Choose what works for you: Listen to calming music, do a relaxation exercise. Prime yourself for pleasant dreams.

☐ **Upload a nature scene to your computer screen.** Bring the natural world into your technological one. Feature a view you love—of a pretty meadow, a sunset vista, or a hammock on a tropical isle—on your laptop screen or as your smartphone wallpaper.

Feel Paradise

Turn your life into a day spa. Years ago, my sister and I were treated to a short stay at a resort in Cabo San Lucas, Mexico. Every day, I'd shower in a tiled room by an open window facing the ocean, then use the moisturizer provided by the hotel. A few months later, I borrowed a friend's lotion and was instantly transported back to that shower by the sea. I quickly bought the same one for myself (it was Aveda's Caribbean Therapy, if you're curious), and for months, every time I lathered it on, I felt calm, happy, and at peace. In the same way, unwind by bringing little moments of spa into your life every day.

- **Find your own spa-like lotion.** Don't just pick the first thing off the shelf. Sniff away until you find a scent or texture that feels luxurious to you.
- **Light candles.** Light a candle in the bathroom while you shower or take a bath.
- **Go fluffy.** Spas love fluffy robes, towels, and washcloths. Get plush at home, too.
- **Import nature.** Make your own strawberry body scrub (mix together about five ripe strawberries, a few tablespoons of olive oil, and about a tablespoon of coarse sea salt), rub some coconut oil on your rough spots before you step into a hot bath, or add a stalk of lucky bamboo in a vase to your countertop.

☐ **Go for an evening walk.** The world is so different after dark. It's an adventure to see yours from a slow stroll down the sidewalk as you listen to the night sounds of crickets, frogs, diners at outdoor restaurant tables, or music from your neighbors. Step outside, under the stars, and take your sweet, strolling time. No destination required.

☐ **Follow the light.** See what the light is doing at different times of the day: A morning glow lighting up the garage. Afternoon luster making shadows of little leaves on the building next door. Golden streaks from the setting sun on the kitchen countertop. Same home, altered vibe, through one single day's path of the sun.

☐ **Put a notepad by your bed.** Sleep issues don't come from lumpy beds; they come from brains that won't shut off. Battle your busy thoughts by downloading them onto paper to deal with tomorrow. Write down tomorrow's to-dos, or that idea you have for a movie, or the inspiring line you can use in your speech. Wipe them off the blackboard of your mind and set them down safely somewhere else.

☐ **Let something go.** A balloon. A fish you've caught but will not eat. A resentment you've carried too long. Exhale and let it leave you, to float off in the wind or down into the depths, taking the heaviness with it.

Be Calm

Invent your own personal calming system. Sometimes a little stress is good for us, mobilizing us into action through the fight-or-flight response of our sympathetic nervous system. But happiness is about balance, so it's also healthy to learn how to engage the parasympathetic nervous system—the rest-and-digest response—that calms you down when you need it. Give yourself a go-to way to relax in thirty seconds, wherever you are. Try:

- **Give yourself droopy bedroom eyes.** Imagine that a hypnotist is telling you that you're getting sleepy, very, very *sleeeepy*. Let your eyelids fall to half-mast, as if they're too tired to stay open.
- **Do twelve seconds of deep breathing.** Inhale through your nose for a count of five, and then exhale through your mouth for a count of seven.
- **Smile like a crazy person for ten seconds.** Research has shown that while happy experiences can make us smile, engaging the smile muscles also sends a message to the brain that we are happy.

☐ **Do one session of progressive muscle relaxation.** Starting with your toes, tense all the muscles as tightly as you can, then completely relax. Work your way up from your feet to the top of your head.

☐ **Conjure your perfect place.** A meditation tape might tell you to "picture a relaxing place." Is yours a shimmering lake? A hilly mountain? A white sand beach at the sea? Know for sure what yours is, and call on it often for peace.

☐ **Take the nap, sleepy.** We're like batteries; we wind down, too. If you're exhausted and you have a comfy place to close your eyes with a few minutes to spare, then take a nap. It's your body's way of saying, "Psst, we need a recharge." So close your eyes, relax, and plug in.

NINE

Confidence

The more you feel **empowered** in your own life, the happier you can be. **Treat** yourself with ideas that will **fortify** your **independent** spirit and help you **flourish** with strength, **wisdom**, and bright, good things.

☐ **Invite yourself on a date.** Take yourself to a play for a Sunday matinee, for a stroll through the state park, to brunch at a French bistro, or to a film on Friday night. It may be quieter than your average date, but you'll be pleased when you realize what easy company you are.

☐ **Shoot a goal.** Knock an air hockey puck into the goal. A basketball swished into the net. A billiard ball in the pocket. A piece of rolled-up paper into the garbage can. Hitting a goal feels good, even from just inches away.

☐ **Name a benefit you've gained from a difficulty you've faced.** Through some bad comes good, and often in unexpected ways. Writer Elizabeth Weingarten wrote in *Slate* magazine, for example, that her life-threatening allergy to tree nuts gave her an unexpected "superpower." Having to question servers in restaurants about ingredients, she said, taught her "to be assertive and persistent . . . to be my own protector and guardian." Find your own superpower, the smooth stone that surfaces beneath a rough experience.

☐ **Remind yourself right now: "I'm more than enough."** Do you ever think, "I'm not hot enough," or "I'm not successful enough," or "I'm not tall enough," or "I'm not cool enough"? Well, there will never be a day you cross that finish line of "enough" on the outside, for it is an imaginary line within you. Today, erase the line. You are *more* than enough. *You are just how you should be.*

☐ **Head to the airport whenever you darn well please.** I like to arrive two hours early; you might like to cut it close. But whatever your choice for the airport—or a concert or movie, for that matter—follow your gut and don't let others influence your timetable. Go when you want and fly free.

☐ **Remove one mirror from your space.** I didn't know how much I checked the mirror in my hallway until I placed a painting there instead. Which is when I realized: If you can't see what you look like, you can't care! Remove a mirror and "see" for yourself. What freedom, to live in your space with one less thought of how you appear.

☐ **Shine a Broadway spotlight on your fear.** Are you anxious about speaking up? Feel awkward ordering on a date? Then free yourself from the pressure by just saying so. You might not be the only one. Admitting it is like opening the cage door and letting the anxiety out. And as soon as you let it go, *you'll* be the one who feels free.

☐ **Power a new machine.** Get behind the controls of something you've never used: a riding lawn mower, a baking mixer, a potter's wheel, a power sander, or a sewing machine. Feel the energy churning under your hands, such possibility at your fingertips.

☐ **Watch the film everyone on earth seems to have seen but you.** I promise: You're not the only one who hasn't seen it. And just think how nice it will be not to have to hear once and for all, "What? *You* haven't seen _____?" You may like it, you may not. But once and for all, you'll have an opinion either way.

☐ **Climb something.** A monument, a mountain, the great steps, a hill. The view from the bottom is good, but your proud, panting view from the top is a well-earned extra.

☐ **Ask yourself: What's the best thing that could happen?** What's the best that could happen—in love, with money, in school, at the car wash? Imagine what could awesomely happen and you might attract interesting circumstances your way.

☐ **Go a day without makeup.** This one, I admit, is easy for the guys. For the rest of us? Take the challenge: For one day, show up for life as is. No mascara. No lipstick. No blow-dryer. Pull back your hair into a ponytail or bobby pin and show your face: clean, bare, fresh and 100 percent fully you.

☐ **Learn how you learn.** Some people learn visually—by seeing it written on paper or performed in front of their eyes. Others retain information better by hearing some-one explain it. Still others pick it up best by using their own hands, by touching the keyboard or driving the route them-selves. Find the technique that seems to suit you, and it will change your learning life forever.

☐ **Put something so "you" on the entrance to your home.** Maybe it's a fun fish mailbox, a kooky sign on your apartment door, a beautiful wreath, or a peaceful welcome plaque you purchased on your travels. Let people know who you are in spirit before they've stepped foot inside the door.

☐ **Throw out your lame socks.** You know the ones: with a hole in the toe, a threadbare heel, or the ones that are all un-elastic-y and sad. Get rid of the socks you push past hoping for one of your *good* pairs. You have to reach in often, right? So make your sock drawer something that makes you and all ten toes really happy.

☐ **Oh, and throw out your lame underwear, too.** One character said it best on an episode of the former ABC television show *Go On* after someone vowed to wear her good underwear for the occasion: "You're a grown-up," the character replied. "*All* your underwear should be good underwear."

☐ **Look it up, once and for all.** I admit it: I only recently learned what "turnkey" meant when talking about move-in-ready real estate. So if there's something that still stumps you (a teetotaler is someone who *doesn't* drink, right?), answer your own question for good.

☐ **Politely disregard an opinion of you.** You're not what other people think of you. You're what *you* think of you.

☐ **Say "I am my own good time."** It's not up to other people if your night is a blast or a bust. Holidays, parties, dates, and group gatherings are just additional channels to help us get there. So the next time you wonder if you'll have fun, say "I am my own good time." Then make it so.

☐ **Read something that would make your literature teacher proud.** Yes, the *whole* thing.

☐ **Plant a perennial flower.** A daffodil, an iris, a yellow yarrow, whatever will be heartiest in your geographical zone. Watch the seasons put it to sleep until spring, when you'll notice again a tiny white bulb or green sprout or a fresh bloom effortlessly rising up that you'd forgotten all about. This is us, this flower, day after day, year after year, bouncing back.

☐ **Watch a documentary.** Peek into another corner of the world. Open your own eyes to how others live and be inspired to see your own life differently—or maybe even to take action within it.

☐ **Memorize a poem.** Small bites of beauty are good for us, little moments lit bright and then gone. Flip to one in a book that reflects how you're feeling. Or look up haikus online that speak to you in a few words. One of my favorite short poems is "The Red Wheelbarrow," by William Carlos Williams. Sixteen words, simply divine.

☐ **Learn to say something positive in another language.** You'll feel growth. You'll impress others. And according to research on language learning, you'll grow your brain! A Swedish study found it grows the hippocampus, involved in spatial navigation and learning new things as well as parts of the cerebral cortex responsible for learning and motor skills. To get you started, try: "everything is beautiful" in Italian: *molto bello*. And "how incredible" in French: *incroyable!*

☐ **Skip it!** Allow yourself one of Monopoly's "Advance to Go" cards in life, and allow yourself to skip straight to the good stuff. If you don't like a chapter in the book, move on to the next one. If you're bored eating dinner, jump ahead to dessert. If you don't have to finish and you really don't want to, skip your way to happy.

☐ **Ask your opposite.** Which shoes should you wear? What job should you take? Which guy should you date? Listen to why *they'd* do what they suggest and get an even fuller understanding of what choice is right for you.

☐ **Learn a new constellation.** Get to know Orion's belt or the shape of Cygnus, the Swan. Then seek it out up above in the right season. It's satisfying to witness the consistency of the universe, rotating around us every day. "Yep, there it is," you can say of a small part of the night sky tucked away in your memory.

☐ **Ignore the dust bunny under the couch.** Or the stain on your shirt. Or the zit on your face. Or the wrinkle on your pants. People simply don't see the small stuff, unless you aim the lens right toward it.

☐ **Seek a new turn on your learning curve.** If you've reached a flattening in your life learning curve, a stall so dull you can't bear it, see what *you* can bring to the situation that will change it. Can you work in a new section? Try a different hobby? Steer right and see what you find.

☐ **Put your envy in perspective.** I envied my friend who has a home like a décor catalog until I realized: She doesn't have *my* best friend, *my* mom, *my* cat's funny "midnight freak-out." Those people you envy don't have what you do: *your* sibling, *your* sense of adventure, *your* laugh, *your* life.

☐ **Forgive your moment of weakness.** We are not purely "strong" or "weak"; staunchly "resilient" or really "not." We ebb and flow with our fortitude, without it making a permanent mark on who we can be. When you need to let go, *it's okay.* Give up, give in, then go to sleep. You can be strong again tomorrow.

☐ **Look for today's four-leaf clover.** Spend an hour actively seeking out lucky things: a green light, a big discount, a good parking spot, a short line at the post office. Good fortune isn't as rare as you think.

☐ **Hammer a nail.** It's so pure, the hammering of one straight nail into wood or a wall. Give yourself the chance to feel that power. If you build it, strength will come.

☐ **Dig to the core of what grates on you.** If you can't stop talking about how much you passionately dislike something, dost thou protest too much? I dated a few people I hadn't liked the first time we met, and still find myself singing whole pop songs I swore I despised. Dig around your dislikes and see what you really might . . . well, love.

☐ **Ask three friends what they think your "friend strength" is. Then use it!** Do they say you're social? Offer to plan their birthday brunch. Empathetic? Offer an ear. Clever? Offer to help them rewrite their online dating profile. When you use what you're good at to help others, you'll get just as much back yourself.

☐ **Go for something "gulp"-worthy.** Leap from the high rock. Walk on the edge. Step into the circle and dance. If your palms are sweating and your heart is pounding, you're probably doing something that's good for you. Because a physical act of bravery can give you emotional strength you never knew you had.

☐ **Use your fists to gain control.** If you want to strengthen your willpower in a moment, strengthen a muscle in your body. Because the body and mind are so intertwined, explains a study published in the *Journal of Consumer Research*, the act of clenching a fist can create more self-control. So if you want to keep from texting that ex or eating the whole pan of brownies (when, really, one row is enough), make a fist and show you really mean it.

☐ **Write a poem.** It's your own private language of how you see things: bright or feisty or craggy or cold. Make it rhyme or not. Make it long or short. Make it yours.

☐ **Don't skim over the hard part.** Years ago, I was writing a story full of conflicting statistics. In trying to avoid poking the bee's nest of confusion, I tried to write around it. "No," said my editor. "Don't skim over the hard part. Just tell us what it is." The same is true for life: If your heart is broken or your passion is floundering, reveal the hard part—the *human* part—and see what happens.

☐ **"Raise your hand" in real life.** When a kid is confused in class, he raises his hand to ask a question. So what's holding us back as adults from essentially doing the same? I've had the most enlightening conversations when I admitted

I didn't have a clue about something, from a political policy, to a football player, to a country I didn't, uh, know existed. It takes strength to ask what might "feel" like a silly question—but remember, there's no such thing.

☐ **Call in your Party Reserve Team.** Have you ever planned an event, then worried if anyone would show up? *Pfft*. Never again—not once you build your Party Reserve Team, that is. Ask two close friends to arrive an hour early, so whether no one else comes—or everyone does—you'll still be ensured a good time.

☐ **Get a lucky charm.** Research out of Germany has found that believing in a lucky charm can enhance your success on tasks both physically and mentally. It's a placebo effect—that confidence from believing in it is doing all the work—but what's the harm in giving yourself a little extra faith? Pack a lucky charm and don't be afraid to use it!

☐ **Don't go through life intent on avoiding the worst.** Pray, instead, that the best will come out of you if the worst hits. You have smarts and strength and resourcefulness to handle anything.

☐ **Face a "never, ever" head-on.** What's something you can never picture yourself doing? Now, answer this: Why not? What's *so* crazy about that thing—running a marathon, going to Africa, getting married—that stops it from being you? Perhaps it's finances or opportunity. But maybe there's something *else* holding you back, a fear that can be healed. Think about it. It could change your ever after.

Be Independent

Live it up when you go solo. Partnerships are wonderful. But our happy point in life is not when we've partnered up; the happy point is when we find where we thrive. So whether you're single or in a romantic relationship, don't miss the great experiences you can have on your own.

- **Get good at little things.** Master picture hanging, plant watering, oil changing, and squeak fixing. With self-sufficiency, there's no such thing as learning too much.
- **Strengthen your friendships.** Reach out to a few others with your goals, fears, and guilty pleasures.
- **Feed your cravings.** Enjoy weird meals, odd movies, television marathons, and dream trips. No compromise required; it's all up to your unique mood.
- **Find your flow.** Get painting, boxing, singing, cooking, building, jogging, or writing. You'll find your flow when you're lost in your own awesome mind.

☐ **Dine out alone.** Yes, out. And yes, *alone*. Let go of the crutches that your friends, kids, or partners give you while you eat, and have a "table for one" meal. Bring a book or sit and people watch at a café, an airport lounge, or a trendy restaurant you've been wanting to try.

☐ **Replace the word "fine" with something stronger.** We usually say, "It's fine" when we're feeling something else, a doubt we'll probably bring up later and pour out. (You know the ol' "Well, I was just *saying* it was fine because I didn't want to make a big deal about it.") But as "hey" is for horses, "fine" is for the feeble. Pick a stronger word than "fine" that says what you *really* mean. It's better to discuss the facts than argue over the undercurrents of what no one is brave enough to say.

☐ **See the good weight you've gained.** I had skinnier thighs ten years ago. But I was also thinner in life experience. While we may have gained weight, we have also gained wisdom. You won't see it on the scale, but it is worth measuring.

☐ **Ask your friends what they're most proud of.** Is it the table they built from scratch? Regaining the use of their injured hand? The business they started with $30 and a bucketful of fearlessness? What someone takes pride in says worlds about who he or she is, and it can set a fire in us to do proud for ourselves.

Be Honest

Tell the truth. I once spent weeks arranging a story interview, only to completely *forget* to call my subject at the appointed time. When she checked in with me, no excuse I could make up seemed good enough, so I went with the truth. "I'm so sorry!" I said. "Three weeks of emails to set this up and I totally just plum forgot." Instead of being angry, though, she commiserated and we had a lovely chat. (Phew!) Honesty not only works, as I learned that day; it's also good for you. Research has found that people report fewer common illnesses like headaches and sore throats during weeks when they have lied less—likely because being honest is healthy for our relationships, and being happy in our relationships leads to better physical health. So tell it like it is. Let people know they can trust you and your word.

- **If you're wrong in a fight** . . . give in. "You're right, I'm sorry" works wonders.
- **If you've screwed up** . . . say "I screwed up."
- **Avoid cliché excuses** about big traffic and slow trains and try, "I left late. I'm a jerk."
- **When someone insists on your honest opinion** . . . offer it.

☐ **Snuggle into the sleeping bag of "uncomfortable."** If life was about being comfortable all the time, we'd be huddled in bed under down blankets all day long! Today, appreciate the other feelings, too—the nervous, anxious, uneasy, upset, uncertain ones. Just sit in the puddle of how it feels *between* the good parts. That stuff doesn't always feel good, but it's on every path to something brilliant.

☐ **Yes, bother.** Why clean up when it's just going to get dirty again? Why fix the hem that no one else will see? Why do it right if you can get away with doing it wrong? Because. Not everything you do will be seen on the outside, but you'll know you've done it from within. Your standards are enough. So next time, make a quality choice.

☐ **Be brave!** You can only be brave by being scared of something in the first place. Otherwise, it's just another step on a normal day. Think of it that way the next time your heart is pounding with panic: Fear isn't there to stop you; it's meant to make you even prouder for pushing past it and taking the chance.

☐ **Throw something as far as you can.** We don't always have a football field of space, but if you find some, use it. Pitch a ball across the park as far as you can. Pick up a rock and hurl it into a pond. It's not the distance that feels good, it's the effort. One hundred and ten percent of all you've got, powered into one hearty shot.

Be Deep

Focus on what matters. I was deeply moved by a story I read about a woman of the Sikh faith, Balpreet Kaur, who was mocked online for dressing out of fashion and letting her facial hair grow. "When I die, no one is going to remember what I looked like," Kaur bravely replied. "However, my impact and legacy will remain: and, by not focusing on the physical beauty, I have time to cultivate those inner virtues and, hopefully, focus my life on creating change and progress for this world in any way I can." Wow, right? From insult comes inspiration. Our outsides fade. But what we pass on lives on.

- **It's not how handsome our faces are that matters . . .** it's how we use our faces to cry and laugh, to express excitement, to show empathy when we mean it.
- **It's not the clothes on our bodies that matter . . .** it's how we use our bodies to tickle, to hug, to run, to carry, to birth, to play, to console.
- **It's not our computers or smartphones that matter . . .** it's how we use them to email, text, share photos, send videos, and connect with the people we love.

☐ **Say no if you really don't want to go!** Because happiness isn't always about saying yes. In fact, research suggests that women who engage in "sociotropy"—the official psychological term for people-pleaser tendencies—are more likely to feel stress and depression, due to feeling overcommitted and resentful. So this time, RSVP with your *own* happiness in mind.

☐ **Give your style a name.** How you want to feel in your clothes is a telling clue of who you are. So answer this: How do you want to *feel* when you're dressed your best? Do you want to feel "classically chic," "bohemian fun," "sporty cool," or "island rad"? Choose the words that feel right, then live up to your personal style in life.

☐ **Toss something that was "the old you."** I've been holding on to jeans I haven't squeezed into in ten years to inspire me to work out. But the truth is, they just make me feel guilty for not fitting into them! Things that don't fit into our current lives only hold us back and keep us from making progress. So toss out a piece of the old you to open up room for the new one.

☐ **Have a naked hour.** Maybe it's just you in your living room with the curtains closed; maybe it's you and your partner playing a game of Uno. Either way, that's *your* birthday suit and you should be darn proud of it.

Be Hopeful

Have a "feel-a-thon." Instead of wishing you had something, imagine—really imagine for fifteen intense seconds—what it would *feel* like if you had it. Feel the swoop in your stomach as if you were riding high in a hot-air balloon. Feel the butterflies you'd get that first time you kiss someone you love. Feel the tingles of being a mom to the baby you dream of having. Because when you focus on what you want to feel instead of what you fear, you open the doors of possibility. The world is profoundly enormous, and what you want is possible if you start seeing it that way. Don't just wish for it; *feel* all your wishes come true.

- *Feel* **what it's like to have a deep, true, compassionate love.** Imagine it: laughing, hugging, cuddling, and gazing into one another's kind, trusting eyes.
- *Feel* **what it's like to live in abundance.** Imagine it: eating, building, moving, traveling, learning, and living a fabulously free and wonderful life.
- *Feel* **what it's like to achieve your dreams.** Imagine it: reaching, daring, going for it, glowing, winning, having, and being the best version of you.

☐ **Ask for autonomy.** We do our best when we feel our actions mean something, that we're not just a weak set of hands on the tug-of-war rope. Ask your boss, your family, your friends, or yourself for a chance to show your strength. Prove to the world that you have it.

☐ **Invite someone who intimidates you out for coffee.** That boss, that classmate, that keynote speaker—they've all been intimidated at times in life, too. If they want to say no, that's on them. But they may say yes, and then you've got yourself some insight, a friend, or a mentor in the making.

☐ **Challenge an assumption.** We all make assumptions about people—from across the street, the room, or the restaurant table. And we may be missing out because of it. Sure, someone may *seem* intimidating, standoffish, or odd. But you won't know if they really are, unless you talk to them and find out for yourself.

☐ **Show your vulnerability.** Like turning a homemade pillow inside out so people can see the stitching, it takes true strength to reveal the messy parts. Admit that you're nervous. Share why you're scared. Acknowledge your loneliness. Peel off the outside perfect layer and let people see the softer side underneath.

☐ **Change how your story ends.** You can't change what's already happened in your life, but you have the power to choose your own adventure from here. Start in the next hour: Date who you want, work how you want, say what you want, love who you want, eat what you want. Then turn to a new page and choose your own adventure all over again tomorrow.

TEN

Grace

Those who **give** back to the **world** and feel their life has **meaning** say they are happier than those who don't. These **generous** ideas will bring out the warm, **kind** person you are in your **heart**. When you give, you receive.

☐ **Say hi to that doggie in the window.** Before pets get love in a real home, they'd benefit from a dose of yours. Play with the animals at the adoption fair. Stop by a local shelter. Visit the cockatoos and bunnies at the pet food store. Show little animals the love of a home, even outside of it.

☐ **Ask an older person for advice.** And—here's the hard part—take it. They don't know your life, but they know *life*. And they may be honored to share what they've learned. Use their past to help your future.

☐ **Have a do-good date.** Instead of your average dinner date, donate your time together to plant a garden, deliver meals to the elderly, or help tutor children after school.

☐ **Leave a little art for someone.** Take inspiration from artist Andy Goldsworthy, who famously forms art from natural materials like leaves, rocks, pinecones, and sand; ephemeral works meant to be washed away by nature. Build a tower of twigs, a circle of shells, a single row of pebbles at the base of a tree. Create beauty that will make others smile, then pass in time.

☐ **Sign up to be an organ donor.** Take the short but vital step of offering what your body will someday no longer need to someone whose body can survive because of it. Don't just live for today; help others live for the future.

☐ **Give away a big bag of stuff.** Clothes. Canned goods. Baby toys. Shoes. Books. Computers. Find the people who need it most—the less fortunate in your area, the military, or a school abroad—and pay it forward.

Be Generous

Do the right thing. My friends and I rent a shack at the beach every summer, and we've created a rule at the house: No matter what time it is, day or night, we will *always* pick each other up and drop each other off at the bus or train station— even for 5 a.m. departures or arrivals after midnight. Favors can sometimes be inconvenient in the moment, but in the long run, it feels good to do the right thing.

- **Pick someone up from the airport.** Be the in-person welcome wagon.
- **Let family stay with you.** It's only 4 days out of 365.
- **Help your coworker** by lifting from their workload when they're overwhelmed.

☐ **Pick up litter in public.** You don't have to be part of a "Clean-Up Day" or a formal volunteer event to toss out the trash in a beautiful place. Or go smaller: Pick up the papers that missed the garbage can on the copy room floor. Take it upon yourself to better the world around you, right now.

☐ **Forgive someone.** Here's an approach that might help: Try to imagine the person they were at age six or eight, when all they wanted was to feel loved and to play on the swings. They have hurt you, but they have also *been* hurt. Forgive the child in them, the pure part of their heart.

☐ **Do it right, Hawaiian style.** Think *kina'ole*, which means doing the right thing, in the right way, at the right time, in the right place, to the right person, for the right reason, with the right feeling . . . the first time.

☐ **Spot someone doing a good deed.** Seek out someone opening a taxi door, lifting a child up for a better view, giving directions, or offering change. And if you can't spot a kind action within ten minutes . . . do one yourself!

☐ **Send a care package.** Have you ever experienced the giddiness of getting a care package—maybe one filled with snacks and stickers as a kid, or a box of chocolate goodies for a holiday? Send one off yourself to a family member far away, to a friend who's moved and misses the local favorites, or to someone in the military who'd appreciate, more than anyone, a little taste of home.

☐ **Grab an extra.** Whenever I buy something for myself that I know my sister is going to love, I've gotten into the habit of grabbing one for her, too. So as soon as she compliments my scarf/bracelet/keychain/pen, I can hand her one of her own. Do this with things you grab on vacation or at home. If you know someone will love the same barbecue rub, children's toy, or bouquet of peonies, snatch one up and pass it along.

☐ **Surprise shovel.** After you shovel your own driveway, shovel for a neighbor who lives on her own, or for a family on vacation who would be thrilled to return, exhausted, and see it already done. Your reward? Peeking out the window to see their glee.

☐ **Offer what you're done with.** Your grocery cart. Your parking spot. The hot sauce on your table. The magazine you've finished reading to the train of people who still have an hour to go.

☐ **Plant a "giving tree."** Plant an extra vegetable, bush, vine, or tree just to give its harvest away. Water it knowing that *those* peaches, cucumbers, squash, or avocados are the ones you'll pile in baskets and give to your friends and neighbors. Like the boy in Shel Silverstein's children's book *The Giving Tree*, they will be happy.

☐ **Deliver a picnic.** Bring a fancy lunch to a new mom who hasn't been able to leave the house. For an ill friend in the hospital, carry in their favorite restaurant meal. Take out, then take it in.

☐ **Pay their way.** Pay the small toll for the car behind you. Pay the parking fee for your friend's car that pulls in after you. Pay the fare for the person stepping onto the bus behind you. Set the ride of kindness into motion.

☐ **Offer to drive an elderly neighbor somewhere.** Ask, "Can I drive you somewhere this week?" It may make their day to get a ride to the market, to church, to bingo. Have car, will travel . . . for the good of others.

☐ **Wash someone's dishes for them.** Suds up the dinner plates for your host and give them a shiny, clean sink to wake up to.

☐ **Be gracious to someone onstage.** Can you imagine tap-dancing, singing, telling jokes, or strumming for an audience, and all you receive are some blank stares in return? Offer the next entertainer you see a thank-you smile or a genuine clap to acknowledge you appreciate they're performing their heart out.

☐ **Stick through someone else's something.** A friend's speech. A neighbor's dance recital. A peer's independent film. Not every movie is an Oscar winner, or every play a hit, but every big effort takes work to make and bravery to release. Show your support by showing up.

☐ **When you hear an ambulance, say a prayer.** The next time you hear a siren or pull over to let an ambulance pass, silently send a prayer of hope and recovery to anyone who is hurt and those who love them.

☐ **Make a "Can I grab you anything?" offer.** If you're at a drive-through, in a hardware store, a spice shop, or IKEA, what can you grab for someone who might need it? Light-

---

Be Empathetic

Understand your loved ones. Seek to understand a person by tuning in to what psychologists call our "family of origin" for answers. Because we all grew up differently, inquiring about the dynamics of the family a person was raised in is key to understanding how they view everything from relationships and money to parenting, chores, and work today.

- **Understand how they see money.** Did their mother clip coupons to put food on the table? Did their father splurge easily on upgrades?
- **Understand their social personality.** Did they grow up in a family where they were criticized by a parent or sibling? Were they in a home where their opinion was valued?
- **Understand how they see relationships.** Did one parent defer to the other in making big decisions? Did their parents have a hostile relationship or a happy bond?

---

bulbs? Toilet paper? Tacos? Even a morning carton of milk for coffee just might make a friend's day.

☐ **Insist that you'll babysit, dog-sit, or plant-sit.** No one likes to ask friends to watch their child or feed their pet— and not everyone has the funds to pay for someone who can. So offer to do it for free. More specifically, *insist*. Force your friends who are new parents out for a date night, or offer to water the plants and feed the cats so your neighbors can have a relaxing weekend away.

☐ **Use your gifts for good.** We are all good at something. Maybe it's measurable—like sewing, building, or dancing—and maybe it's something more subtle—like warmth or an ability to communicate. Whether you're a teacher, a preacher, a singer, or a safe shoulder to lean on, use your gifts for good.

☐ **Plant a memory garden.** Plant a flowering bush, a rose garden, or a fruit tree in honor of a loved one. Then watch it bloom with pretty reminders of the life they lived.

☐ **Do something small that changes the world.** It's not one person who changes the world, it's *all* of us. Sign a petition that defends civil rights. Donate money to a friend's walk-a-thon for cancer research. Your vote, your donation, your signature, and your time matter because small actions can have a very big impact.

☐ **Have a gift-gathering day.** Choose a day to gather gifts. Maybe you'll shop for a few birthdays at once. Maybe you'll pluck wildflowers from the garden and give them to your two favorite people. Maybe you'll paint postcards for your family members or find the perfect housewarming gift. When you think, "Who can I get a present for?" some surprising people might come to mind.

☐ **Use a recyclable bag at the market.** That's one plastic bag that won't end up wrapped around wildlife in the ocean, that won't get buried in the clean, damp earth. Use the same bag twice . . . even just once. Give the earth some peace.

☐ **Laugh at someone's joke.** We're not all comedians, and we're not all meant to be! But telling a joke is like stepping onstage with the spotlight all on you. So be "the good guy" and be gracious. Applaud them for trying with your best chuckle.

☐ **Move your muscles for a cause.** You don't need money to raise money. Sometimes you just need your two feet or whatever can propel you toward a finish line. It's healthy for your body, your soul, and the people you're helping by reaching out.

☐ **Be the pebble that ripples the water around you.** According to research out of Emory University, reaching out to help others triggers activity in the same areas in our brains associated with pleasure and reward. So open a door, carry a box, give up your seat for an elder. Be kind. Be helpful. Be generous. The ripples will carry on.

☐ **Name one way you were fortunate this week.** Did you have a close call with another car at an intersection and still drive away unscathed? Did you manage to keep your job during downsizing? Get a hearty rain before you had to water the lawn? This week, you were probably luckier than you think.

☐ **Pull the hope card.** Do you know what the survival rate of U.S. airplane accidents is? According to the National Transportation Safety Board, it's actually 95 percent. In other words, your chances are overwhelmingly good. Imagine the same is true of other seemingly "hopeless" things: Maybe there *is* a road without traffic; maybe you *can* afford a new washer; maybe you *will* find love. Hope is to success like oxygen is to a flame: It burns when there is room for it to grow.

Be Kind

Be the welcoming face in the crowd. Sunshine and smiles can be deceiving. We never know when someone is covering up pain, stress, or sadness with a positive spin—and we never know when our small act of kindness can be just the thing that gets someone else through a rough day. You may not know someone else's story, but your small kindness might make a difference. Maybe you can . . .

- **Invite someone** different to sit next to you in a meeting.
- **Say "No rush at all"** to quell the panic of a harried server who's in the weeds.
- **Happily hold the elevator** door open for someone who is still a short jog away.
- **Give a deliberate smile** to the person in the ticket booth.
- **Add an extra tip** for the person who washed your car.

☐ **Donate to those who have nothing.** Every year, a friend of mine builds holiday gift bags for the homeless: She packs forty bags full of tissues, socks, hand wipes, cough drops, water bottles, and snacks she collects with her friends, and delivers the bags to people in need. Simple gifts still mean a lot.

☐ **Let someone's boss know how much they've helped you.** I recently spoke with a customer service representative who was so kind and efficient with my computer issue that the call was actually a pleasant experience. After I hung up, I wished I'd gotten her name and let her superiors know what a class act she'd been. If someone is putting a good face on their company, make their day—and maybe their raise—by letting their boss know.

☐ **Rubberneck with utter gratefulness.** We can't seem to avoid rubbernecking when we pass an accident. So as long as we're crawling past a fender bender, take a moment to remember: You are okay and driving and safe. Give thanks for that.

☐ **Ask for help.** Asking makes you vulnerable, but in the most beautiful, humanizing way. Because when we really see each other, we want to help each other.

☐ **Be patient with someone else's speed bump.** Maybe it's a client's hearing problem that makes you repeat yourself; maybe it's a relative's slow, fearful driving that makes the trip longer; or maybe it's a roommate's inability to grasp a concept quickly. Put yourself in their shoes: Perhaps the very thing that's making you angry may be something that's been bugging or embarrassing them for years. Be patient, for them and for you.

☐ **Choose one regret and *let it go*.** So you said it. Or you went for it. Or you were too chicken to make a move, send a signal, or grab someone by the shirt collar and kiss them. Let it go. Things worked out the way they did for a reason—the *right* reason. This time, it simply wasn't meant to be.

☐ **Write your legacy.** What, at the end of your life, would you want to read about how you lived? Answer this of your future self: She/he left behind this legacy that cannot be denied: _____.

☐ **Let a grudge go.** Holding a grudge is like carrying a brick from a demolition in your backpack; for even though the debris of the original experience has been cleaned up, you're still weighing yourself down. Unzip the backpack, find forgiveness deep within you, and leave the brick behind. You'll feel lighter without the load.

☐ **Give someone the benefit of the doubt.** That lady who cut ahead of you at the meat counter? Work up a reason for her unbearable behavior—*imaginary or not*—to get your patience, tolerance, or understanding into gear. Maybe she had to use the bathroom. Maybe she had to bring food to her sick child. Maybe her parking meter was expiring. She'll be gone soon, so this one time, let her go.

☐ **Send a follow-up to a doctor/service person.** My cousin Lauren is a nurse who adores getting follow-up letters from patients talking about how far they've come. We think that because we step into people's lives for just a minute that we

Be Enthusiastic

Be happy for someone else's good news. My father was recently granted a "Senior Wish" by the Wish of a Lifetime organization, and was sent on a "zero gravity" flight where he got to float like an astronaut in space. What a blast, right? But what was most interesting was how much he said the excitement of his friends and family amped up his own. "It made me think," he said, "that it takes an extraordinary level of generosity to be genuinely excited for a friend who has good fortune. I think someone has to be a really unselfish and giving person to be able to do that." What a beautiful idea. And science supports it. In a 2010 study out of the University of Rochester, researchers found that when people engaged in "capitalization"—sharing good news with others—it made the event more exciting and promoted trust and closeness in the relationships. So rather than chase your own excitement today, get excited about someone *else's* success. Enthusiasm is a gift.

- *Congratulate* **their good news.** With a card, flowers, or an email.
- *Celebrate* **their good news.** With a lunch or an after-work margarita.
- *Ask them for details about* **their good news.** Request photos, and insist on updates in the future.
- *Support* **their good news.** Share the news online, donate money to their cause, or cheer them on.

are well forgotten, but we may linger in their minds forever. It would be great gift to tell a doctor, nurse, therapist,
or teacher who has helped you how you're doing—and a
powerful incentive for them to keep helping others the very
same way.

☐ **Give it your best.** Even if it's not right for someone else, if
your performance passes the test of what *you* know you can
do, then you've done proud by the most important person
in the equation: yourself.

Epilogue

Invite the Good Stuff In

One hot summer afternoon, my friend Laura and her husband David heard an unexpected knock on their front gate in Venice, California. When Laura opened the gate, she was surprised to find a group of young boys and girls from the neighborhood, in baseball hats and surf shorts.

"Hi," said one of them. "We were looking for people in the neighborhood who might have a pool and we heard you had one. We wanted to know if we could come swimming."

When Laura told me this story, she turned to me at this point and asked, "Can you believe it? Isn't that crazy?"

"Very," I said. But I was on the edge of my seat because this story could have gone either way—and I didn't know if she meant it was "crazy good" or "crazy not."

"So?" I had to ask. "Did you let them in?"

"What?" she said with disbelief. "Of *course* I let them in!" Laura was so impressed with the gumption of those kids that she got the okay from their parents and spent the next few hours laughing along as the kids did cannonballs into the pool.

I love that story. Because we have so many moments every day like this, where *we* are standing at the gate of happy opportunities. And it's up to us if we're going to close the door or wave it on in.

Life, after all, is letting out its **plush** carpet and inviting us along for the **ride**. It's teeming with textures and colors, from shiny **balloons** to green **grasses** to **calm** shades of the sea, **swinging** like a **hammock** on the horizon. Life is about **family** who **holds** us when we want to let go; **lovers** who warm us with **hugs** and with **kisses**; friends who bring **healing** with buckets of **laughs**. It's waves to neighbors, **cuddles** with our **pets**, pats on the back, and **high-fives** after a goal. It's **raindrops** in the spring **tickling** our **cheeks**, a summer sun **beaming** onto our lashes, autumn leaves **dancing** under our feet, and white swaths of winter **snow**. It's **flowers** blooming and **fruits** dropping, **icicles** dripping and water flowing. It's **bubble** baths and **champagne**; it's **camping** tents and corn on the **grill**; it's magic and mystery, hard **work** and good **play**. Life is about bearing the weight of the hard times by leaning on the **support** of the good ones.

The fact is, there's no expiration date on happy living, and it's never too late to begin. Because you don't have to overhaul your life to feel better about the one you have. It's the small things that matter the most in how you feel. Happiness is a choice placed in front of you again and again. But don't just look ahead of you to the big things. Look down at what you're walking on, look back at where you've been, and look beside you to see the brilliance of all that's around you. Wring the juice out of every beautiful day.

From now on, start putting those delicious things you want at the top of your to-do list. Make your happiness a priority. Each day, after all, is a brand-new start, a clean blackboard full of possibility. So find your own "happy captures" in the special moments. Open the gate and invite all the good things in.

Acknowledgments

A big thank-you to my incredible literary agent, Laurie Abke-meier, who is always brimming with great ideas, warm encourage-ment, and who makes me feel like I'm the only author on your roster. (Wait . . . I *am*, right?) Beside her on the podium stands my amazing editor, Marian Lizzi. Thank you, Marian, for giving me the freedom and the faith to let these pages unfold on their own, and for your wise editing hand that is always, always right; you made creating this manuscript officially fun! For you both, I am lucky. I'd also like to thank the rest of the team at Perigee, including Nellys Liang, the designer, for creating a cover so cheer-ful it keeps making me smile; Emma Hinkle, for taking on the copyediting challenge of this book; Ann Marie Damian, for her enthusiasm along with her proofreading; and Lauren Becker, for her assistance throughout.

I'd also like to thank my family, my friends, and the new people I met who helped contribute to this book. For months, I asked people about the little things that made big differences in their lives, and every time I heard someone respond, "Ooh! I know something that makes me happy!" it made my heart sing. (By the way, I recommend this even if you're not writing a book about it: Asking what makes *other* people happy does wonders for your mood.) Some people in particular deserve a big thank-you, including my friends in Venice and in New York, especially Todd Bush, Yvonne Cheoun, Patty Bilotti, Jenn Gardiner, Kerry Cushman, Laurie Sandell, Ryan O'Nan, Brandon Young, Jeff Anderson, Jennifer Schwarz, Amy and Charlie Langella, Lisa Kay, Mark Ellwood, Rich Fair, Beth Greenwald, Ellen D. Williams, Leslie Sloan, Danika and Dan, Sharon and Nuri, and Laura Doss—you've all inspired something in these pages and I feel lucky to have you in my life.

To my friend and photographer Phillip Graybill, thank you for bringing this book to life for me on video, as only you could. Big thank-yous also go to Pam Clinkard; Jenn, Andy, and Sophia Ryan; Dee, Riley, and Grace Quinn; Maggie, Thomas, and Seamus Casey; the Weigels; the Bucklers; Courtney Hard; and Mike Verna.

A big thanks to Eric Gordon for being such a talented, funny, and easygoing whiz on the web for me. It's always a joy.

Thank you to my mother, my father, my sister Liz, and Sarah Blanch. Mom, an additional thanks for helping me get some of the psychology reporting right. Thank you to Silvia and Mariana. And thank you to the rest of my family: the Spencers, the McAvoys, the Reeds, the Petits, the Alberos, and the Bengoleas.

An enormous thank-you goes to my husband, Gustavo, who patiently listened as I ran my bright ideas by him. *Again*. And who continues to keep me laughing, fed, and feeling loved. You're the bomb, baby.

And thank *you*: You who have picked up or downloaded or are listening to this book. You who have read my posts on thelifeoptimist.com, who are part of my Vitamin Optimism community, who interact with me on Facebook and Twitter. You who comment and query and send me personal notes to let me know that you're reading what I'm writing. For these I always feel a happy burst of joy.

Gratitude, I'm swimming in it.

About the Author

Amy Spencer is a Los Angeles–based magazine journalist and the author of two previous books: *Bright Side Up: 100 Ways to Be Happier Right Now* (Perigee, 2012), which was recommended by *O, the Oprah Magazine*; and *Meeting Your Half-Orange: An Utterly Upbeat Guide to Using Dating Optimism to Find Your Perfect Match* (Running Press, 2010), which was called "the ultimate pep talk" by *Harper's Bazaar*. Amy grew up in New York, and now lives in Venice, California, with her husband. For more information, visit her website at amyspencer.com.